PENGUIN BOOKS

WHAT MEN DON'T TELL WOMEN

Roy Blount, Jr., is from Georgia and lives in western Massachusetts. He is a contributing editor of *The Atlantic*, writes for many other magazines as well, and is a frequent guest on "A Prairie Home Companion." His previous books include *Crackers* and *One Fell Soup*, also available from Penguin.

What Men Don't Tell Women

ROY BLOUNT, JR.

PENGUIN BOOKS

PENGUIN BOOKS
Viking Penguin Inc., 40 West 23rd Street,
New York, New York 10010, U.S.A.
Penguin Books Ltd, Harmondsworth,
Middlesex, England
Penguin Books Australia Ltd, Ringwood,
Victoria, Australia
Penguin Books Canada Limited, 2801 John Street,
Markham, Ontario, Canada L3R 1B4
Penguin Books (N.Z.) Ltd, 182–190 Wairau Road,
Auckland 10, New Zealand

First published in the United States of America by Little, Brown and
Company, Inc., in association with The Atlantic Monthly Press 1984
Published in Penguin Books by arrangement with Little, Brown and Company,
Inc., in association with The Atlantic Monthly Press 1985
Reprinted 1986

Parts of this book have previously appeared in the following publications: *The
Atlantic, Esquire, Gentleman's Quarterly, HCA Companion Magazine, Los
Angeles Herald Examiner, Madison Avenue, The New York Times Book
Review, Outside, Playboy, TWA Ambassador, Vanity Fair, Vogue.*

"Blue Yodel No. 10"
Words and Music: Jimmie Rodgers
Copyright 1932 by Peer International Corporation
Copyright renewed by Peer International Corporation
Used by permission
All rights reserved

LIBRARY OF CONGRESS CATALOGING IN PUBLICATION DATA
Blount, Roy
    What men don't tell women.
    I. Title.
PN6162.B617   1985   814'.54   84-26568
ISBN 0 14 00.7788 X

Printed in the United States of America by
R. R. Donnelley & Sons Company, Harrisonburg, Virginia
Set in Electra

To Ennis,
before she goes off and leaves her old dad

Contents

I DIDN'T DO IT

Introduction

What Men Don't Tell Women

Got me a pretty momma,
Got me a bulldog too.
Got me a pretty momma,
Got me a bulldog too.
My pretty momma don't love me,
But my bulldog do.

— Jimmie Rodgers, "Blue Yodel No. 10"

I'm . . . No, I won't tell you what I am.

— Henry Kissinger, interviewed by Oriana Fallaci

WOMEN probably think that what men do tell women is bad enough. What is to be gained by telling of such things as Flower Guilt, or Why on Earth Female Dogs Do That, or The Toilet-Seat Issue's Unspoken Crux, or Why You Can't Confess Fidelity. Secrets have reasons. And yet I feel impelled to lay these things before the public, which includes women. It is because of a vision I had at the *Ladies' Home Journal*.

For me the *Ladies' Home Journal* has always had a *musky* quality. It was a prime source of my earliest and most effluvial sex education. When I was a boy, nothing off-color came into our home except Moonbeam McSwine, whose languidly heaving surface, in "Li'l Abner," was veiled by nothing but a tattered — or rather *peeling* — vestige of dirndl and splotches of mud, and who spent her time lolling with hogs. I now trace certain unhygienic dreams of my childish nights back to Moonbeam McSwine, and although Al Capp went sour toward the end of his days and always

3

had a flawed ear for dialect (*yo'* is short not for "you," as Capp would have it, but for "yore," as in "yo' momma"), I am grateful to him.

But my mother subscribed to the *Ladies' Home Journal*, and that was something else. Inside stuff. More than I felt was wise for me to know about, and yet I wanted to know. There were certain ads. ("Modess . . . Because." Because *what? What* because what?) The "Tell Me, Doctor" column. And a regular feature called "Can This Marriage Be Saved?" (Marriage can be *lost?* Marriage? As in marriage that involves parents for instance and, say, little kids for example and, for instance, me — *can be in jeopardy?*) The *Ladies' Home Journal* evoked the way my parents' bed smelled when I climbed in with them in the morning. The primal funk. The gene-pool frowst. It smelled appalling. But homey. It must be saved.

I am not talking about any kind of specific whiff or anything specific that might have been going on in there. What kind of person do you think I am? I'm talking about the whole grave cohabitational bouquet. Books ought to be full of conjugal sheets.

Ironically enough, I was all set to call this book *Clean Sheets.*[1] Then the *Ladies' Home Journal* invited me to come up and discuss story ideas. I welcomed the notion of a writing project wholesome enough to console my late mother, who taught me to read the way lions teach their cubs to pounce, and who never got over the fact that I once wrote about orgasms for *Cosmopolitan.* (That what I wrote was a spoof does not seem to have registered very clearly either with *Cosmopolitan* — see my book *One Fell Soup*, available in stores — or with that Sunday-school classmate of my mother who felt obliged to show the article to her. What I don't understand is, why was anybody in my mother's Sunday-school class reading *Cosmopolitan?*)

1. *Or, My Mind Is All Made Up (But You Can Hop on In).*

But when I went to the offices of the *Ladies' Home Journal*, I learned that it had become a hard-hitting magazine proud of taking on burning controversial topics. (As if there were ever a topic more burning than "Can This Marriage Be Saved?") The editors I talked to — two women of evident dynamism — wanted to know what I thought of the New Woman.

I liked these editors fine and was all for coming to terms with them. But I didn't know what to say about the New Woman. I still don't. I am sitting here, now, trying to think of something to say about the New Woman, in all candor and even desperation, and I can't. And I couldn't then.

So the topic shifted, slightly, to my marriage. I must have blurted something about my marriage. Soon one of the editors was exclaiming, " 'Fifties Man Married to Sixties Woman!' Write us something about that!" My blood ran cold. I said I didn't want to.

"*Why not?*" they said. Well, I said, would *they* want to write about their marriages in a magazine? "We do it all the time!" they said.

We moved on. I let it slip that I had a seventeen-year-old daughter. " 'An Open Letter to My Daughter: Is Youth Wasted on the Young?'!" they exclaimed. I said I didn't want to write an open letter to my daughter in a magazine. They seemed incredulous. I began to mope. Right there in a room with New Women.

"Okay, how about this," one of the editors tried. "We had a writer who was going to do this, but he never did. How about 'What Men Don't Tell Women'!"

Annnnngangang. My head swam.

"Wh . . . why would *I* tell?" I asked weakly. Their incredulity mounted.

"I mean . . . ," I said, "like . . . Tell what?"

"For instance!" one of them said. "Physical Attractiveness Is Important!"

"Ahnh?" I replied.

5

"What men don't tell women is that men *do* look for physical appearance in a woman!"

"W . . . Women don't *know* that?" I asked.

Frankly, it has always seemed to me that women have *at least* as pronounced a sense of the importance of a woman's appearance as men do — hence whole industries; but I was damned if I was going to say that.

"That Men *Are* Attracted to Pretty, Dumb Women!" they said.

"Well . . . ," I said, beginning to feel like an American critic of American foreign policy enfolded by foreign critics of American foreign policy. ". . . I don't know that I'd put it that way. In *fact*, I'm beginning to see more and more *women* my age showing up somewhere with cute young towheaded guys with no stomachs who never heard of Edward G. Robinson."

Actually I did not have in mind, very firmly, a single specific instance of this phenomenon; but I felt there was a case to be made along those lines and I had to say something. "And if being attracted to pretty, dumb members of the opposite sex is a peculiarly male trait," I said, "then why do so many women love Elvis? *Everybody* is attracted, prima facie, to pretty members of the opposite sex, or of whatever sex they're attracted to, and why not? And there's something to be said for being attracted to people who can't outsmart you."

I was overstating my case. I wasn't at all sure I *had* a case and I was overstating it. I have a tendency sometimes to start saying things I don't necessarily actually think, because I don't want people to leap too soon to conclude that I can't possibly think what I think they think I can't possibly think.

Fortunately, I didn't say some of those things about attractiveness out loud. Much of what I uttered to the *Ladies' Home Journal*'s editors, I would imagine, had the ring of well-intentioned but pained moaning sounds.

But pained moaning sounds have reasons. The more I

6

thought about it, after leaving the *Ladies' Home Journal*, the more I realized that I had been writing about What Men Don't Tell Women all my life. In my head or out. If there is anything this book, for instance, is full of, it is things that men don't tell women. Also things that sick people don't tell the well, things that Southern hosts don't tell Northern guests, things that authors don't tell readers, things that hardly anyone will tell anyone about money, things that all too few people tell all too many people who wear hats, and so on. But especially things that men don't tell women.

Men don't tell women these things for various reasons.

1. The things in question may not be true.
2. It is better to keep one's mouth shut and be thought a pig than to open it and oink.
3. There is a certain pleasure in holding certain considerations close to the chest.
4. When there is a topic that might complicate a situation in which a woman is pleased for a man to hold *her* close to his chest, a man does not want to mess with it.
5. It is hard to be manly while making pained moaning sounds.
6. Men, whether or not they have the Right Stuff, have never quite gotten a secure grip on the concept of the Wrong Thing.

But I am an American! I believe in freedom of information! And I have never entirely emerged from the intersexual spell cast on me by intimations I gleaned from the *Ladies' Home Journal* in my newtlike early youth.

Need men and women forever be two separate peoples? Can't there be a link? I decided to give this book the title I have given it. Then I decided to prize apart the book's intricately interlocking pieces and insert certain scraps of testimony, from men of many stripes, revealing for the first time the things that men don't tell. I have called these revelations blue yodels, in tribute to Jimmie Rodgers, the Singing Brakeman, who made an art of the pained moaning sound.

One thing I have found myself unable to reveal is what happened on a certain date that I had many years ago with a cheerleader (see "Secrets of Rooting," page 82). I will say this: It would never have happened if I had been able to tell her something.

Where'd You Get That Hat?

BLUE YODEL 1
JOSEPH

I just came from this Men and Masculinity Workshop. Rose has completed assertiveness training and she said if she was going to continue relating to me in a broader sense I needed to go through tenderness training and claim my wholeness. She said, "Won't it be nice? We'll hang yours over the lowboy right next to mine." She has her assertiveness certificate up there. This workshop gives you one in tenderness.

It met in the Pierce High gym. We sat cross-legged on the floor to break down our stereotype image of how men sit. And we related our feelings while empathizing.

We learned how men have lost their aliveness in relationships because we have been programmed from an early age to always be in control. Alec was our counselor in getting us to open up. Alec said we had always wanted to be tender, but the society told us we couldn't be, but the rapidly growing men's movement was changing that.

We have to acknowledge that we have always been programmed that men have to always be the strong ones. And instead of using women as a dumping ground for our feelings, we have to not be isolated from other men. Alec told us to put our arm around the next man.

I put my arm around this one man, Neil. He said he was working on getting over his aversion to listening to women talk on the phone. He was getting into nonobjective phone conversation, where you talked to hear the other person's voice. Also talking long-distance without any sense of time.

He said it relaxed him. He said his problem came from his father always yelling for everybody in the family to get off the phone for Christ's sake. It took him a long time to realize that relaxing on the phone wasn't sacrilegious. He said he heard there was a way you could apply for a grant to pay your phone bill.

This other man, Jerry, opened up to the group and said his father was not a feeling, emotional man. This other man with a name like Uli said his father wasn't either.

There were these teenage kids coming into the gym bouncing a basketball.

Then Neil said he had something to say he'd never told anybody. He said he walked past his parents' bedroom one morning on his way to breakfast and instead of being at the breakfast table already his father was lying there in the bed still, crying. His mother was burning bacon. Alec asked Neil how this made him feel. Neil said it was why he lost his erection every time he thought of bacon.

Alec said see, that was that whole male myth.

I wished I had my arm around Uli or Jerry instead. What I really wished was that Alec would hurry up and give us our certificates. I could feel Neil tensing up to tell something else. But then these teenage kids said they had the gym.

Alec said no, we had the gym for another half hour.

These kids said no, they had the gym now. Some of them were over messing with Alec's papers and laughing. Alec went and got his papers.

One of the kids said to Alec, "Hey, what's your problem, man?"

Alec said his problem was all men's problem, grappling with changing roles. He asked the kids if they'd like to sit in on the rest of the session.

The kid with the ball was dribbling real hard right next to me and Neil where we were sitting cross-legged on the floor. And then Neil stood up and started telling about how we were trying to become whole people and the kid bounced the ball off Neil's nose.

And then the kids started pounding on all of us while we were getting un-cross-legged and our arms untangled and Neil stole the ball and drove half the court and missed a lay-up. I thought that was pretty cool, if he'd hit it. And the kid Neil stole the ball from pulled out a knife and we left the gym.

We stood outside on the steps. Neil was bleeding. Alec pointed out to us that the kids were caught up in the whole male myth, and we had gotten something out of the experience. He suggested we take turns helping Neil stop bleeding.

So we did, and Neil said his father always accused him of not playing tough when he was hurt. He said one time he had a sprained ankle in the CYO basketball championship and his father made him tape it up and play. "I was eleven," he said. "My father said, 'Be a Marine.'" And Neil missed four lay-ups and his team lost. Neil said he missed lay-ups to prove something to his father.

Then I said, "Well, can we have our certificates?" They were all jumbled up and when Alec got them straight and handed them out, somebody had written FAGIT in big letters on mine.

How will I tell Rose?

How to Visit the Sick

BOUNDING into the room is wrong. Hospitalized people do not like to be bounded in upon. The first thing visitors should see as they step off the elevator is the following sign.

PLEASE DO NOT
TRY OUR PATIENTS BY

1. Bounding in upon them.
2. Creeping in upon them.
3. Being festive.
4. Being grave.
5. Saying, "You look *fabulous!*"
6. Saying (if the patient's name is Vern McGiver), "Oh! Excuse me! I was looking for Vern McGiver's room. I . . . Vern! *Is that . . . you!?*"
7. Telling obvious jokes. For instance, if the patient has had an operation on his or her colon, you may be sure that he or she has heard all the punctuation jokes by now.

But there is no way to squeeze onto one sign all the things that hospital visitors should bear in mind. Some people assume that just by visiting someone who is sick, they are doing a heartwarming thing. That is like assuming that just because you are walking out onto a stage, you are doing an entertaining thing. A person in a hospital bed is often tempted to take advantage of his position (whose advantages are few enough) by cutting into visitors' conversation sharply with: "If somebody doesn't say something *interesting* pretty soon I'm going to hemorrhage."

But he doesn't want to deprive his visitors — call them the Bengtsons — of the chance to feel warmhearted. So he doesn't complain.[1] He just lies there, biding his time until the day when he is up and around and the Bengtsons aren't, and he can visit *them* in a hospital and spill their ice water on their pillows. And the Bengtsons, of course, will have to say, "Oh that's all right! Don't worry!"

One of the burdens of the hospitalized person is that he is, in a sense, the host, and must be gracious to the well. Even though the well often go too far in playing down the seriousness of the patient's complaint: "What you've been through is nothing! My sister had *both* of hers taken out *with no anesthetic*."

Or they play it up too much: "You poor thing. I could no more have borne up under this terrible thing the way you have than . . . Of course, I don't think the full impact of it has hit you yet."

Or they claim too much expertise with regard to the patient's complaint: "Oh, no, no, that's not right at all. What you've actually had removed is *urethral* stones. My aunt had the same thing and I did some research on it to fill her in. You see, your trouble is too many cola drinks. Probably been going on for years. So that a kind of fine brown sediment . . ."

1. The careful reader will note that sometimes my pronouns imply that every person in the world is male, and sometimes that he isn't. When I go out of my way to avoid saying something like, "The trouble with nuclear conflagration is that it will leave man with no sense of his sociometric place" (by saying, "The trouble with nuclear conflagration is that it will leave a person with no sense of his sociometric place, or hers either"), it is because I am suffering from Pronoun Guilt. The question of sexism in pronouns is one that deeply concerns me, since that is the kind of guy I am. I have invented new pronouns, none of which I will cite here because there is nothing quite so funny-looking as a new pronoun. I have devised hermaphroditic characters named Heshie and Sheehy, who have failed to find favor as pronoun replacements. Man has yet to deliver himself from Pronoun Guilt.

Or they are too innocent: "Where exactly *is* the prostate, anyway?"

What are some guidelines to appropriate visitor behavior?

Be sensitive, but not to a fault. Say you are telling a story about frogs. It is better to go ahead and use the word "croak" than to stop at "croa—" and bolt from the room.

Bring gossip. Preferably gossip about people other than the patient. But do not preface such gossip with something like, "Be grateful you're in here. If you were able to work you'd probably be getting fired like Morris Zumer."

Bring anecdotes that make interns and nurses look foolish. Once, in an emergency ward, an intern was trying to deal with a patient who had delirium tremens. "It's your imagination!" the intern insisted. The patient seized him by the necktie so ferociously that the intern could neither breathe nor break the patient's grip. The intern cried out for a nurse, who arrived. "Get . . . scissors . . . cut . . . tie," the intern gasped. The nurse briskly left the room, returned with scissors, pounced, and snipped off the intern's tie — the loose end.

That is a story someone told me in a hospital once, and I enjoyed it. It may not be perfect for every patient. Some patients may prefer quieter stories. Others may have delirium tremens, in which case entertainment is the last thing they need. Every patient is different. But there are three rules that apply to visitors in every case:

- Don't bring hand puppets.
- Don't, even as a "hoot," serve a subpoena.
- Don't get up under the bed and bump around for any reason.

Are you reading this in someone's hospital room? Can it possibly have been left, on purpose, where you would find it? If by any chance you found it under the patient's bed, please get out from under there.

And now please let the patient watch "Family Feud" in peace.

BLUE YODEL 2

KEN

I know this guy, says he has Flower Guilt.

"What?" I say.

He says, "Let's face it: Men don't like flowers."

I say I like flowers.

"Okay," he says. "You like flowers. But you don't love flowers."

"I don't know," I say.

"But you aren't moved by flowers," he says.

"I really like planting zinnias," I say.

"Ah!" he says. "Sure. Delving in the ground. Improving your property. But you don't like getting flowers."

"I guess I don't. Because it would mean I was in the hospital."

"Exactly," he says. "But women like getting flowers."

I say that's true.

"Women love getting flowers. Women are moved when they get flowers. All women. Every woman. Sending flowers to a woman is like . . . heroin to them."

"Well . . . ," I say.

"Okay. But you see my point. My point is, all a man has to do is call a florist — 'Dozen roses, MasterCard number so-and-so, address such-and-such' — and he has done something that a woman will perceive as sweet."

"So what's wrong with that?"

"To a woman, having flowers sent to her is thoughtful. To a man, sending flowers is a way of being thoughtful without putting any thought into it. It's like foreign aid."

I told him I wasn't sure I saw the connection there.

"Okay, forget that," he says. "My point is, when you can melt a woman by doing something that doesn't involve any intrinsic emotion on your part, detachment sets in. Dissociation. Guilt. I send my wife flowers every couple of weeks. A computer could do it. It makes her happy. It makes her happy." He has this pained look. "I'm glad she's happy. But . . ."

"Okay," I say. "So why don't you send Shana" — that's his wife — "why don't you send Shana something thoughtful that does require thought?"

"Because that's how I always get in trouble."

What Authors Do

I AM not the kind of person who feels right about calling himself "a writer," even. It sounds like something you would assert, falsely, in a singles bar. (A friend of mine once asked a young woman what she did. "I'm a novelist," she said. "Really?" he replied. "Would I have heard of any of them?" "I haven't finished it yet," she said.) I'll bet Jesse James, when asked what his line of work was, never said, "I'm a desperado." He probably said, "Oh, something in trains."

But job description does come up. I remember once I walked through a door while poking around in a journalistic capacity backstage at a country music show. Actually my mind was not on the poking so much as on turning a sentence, then in an early development phase, that I thought frankly might buff up pretty nice. "Are you an artist?" someone asked. "Well . . . ," I said in all modesty. Then I saw what he was driving at. I had walked through the wrong door.

Years passed. Then, the other morning at a pancake breakfast, someone — a member of the general public — gave me a funny look and asked, out of the blue, "Are you an author?"

The world shifted for me at that moment.

Hitherto, I had thought of being an author as an *occasional* thing, like being the groom. I was not *working* this pancake breakfast, I was just there to eat. Was I going to have to start living . . . an author's life?

I don't think writers ever say "author." Publishers do, but that is just one more reason why the old question so often arises: What exactly, other than absentmindedness, can the publishing industry and writers ever have imagined they had in common?

What is the difference between an author and a writer? A writer, as we know, writes; an author has written. What does an author *do*? Auth? Authorize? An author authors. But never in the present tense. No one says, when asked what he or she is doing, "I'm authoring." The *Oxford English Dictionary* cites, from Chapman's *Iliad*, "The last foul thing Thou ever author'dst." The *OED* does not explain how "author'dst" is pronounced, but I imagine the full quotation is either

> *Thou mak'st appearances, through the mist*
> *Of the last foul thing Thou ever author'dst*

or

> *Thou goest on Carson; we bog down amidst*
> *The last foul thing Thou ever author'dst.*

Writer derives from various ancient verbs meaning "to tear, to cut, to scratch, to wear by rubbing." Before English got *write, wrote* and *written* right, it tried wryte, vryte, vryet, wryt, wrighte, wreitte, wreat, wrait, wraet, vreet, wrijte, wroite, wreyte, whryte, wrythe, wreyt, wrytte, vryt, vriht, wrygth, wryght, writte, vrit, wret, wrette, wrete, wreit, ureit,

19

wireete, vrait, wrat, whrat, vrat, wart, wratte, wraite, wrayt, wraat, wrot, wrotte, wroate, wroght, wroot, wroott, wrout, wryton, writun, wrytyn, wreotan, wreoton, wreten, ywriten, ywriton, ywritein, ywryten, ywrytyn, uuriten, vrityn, wyrtyn, vyrtyn, whryttyn, vrutten, vreittin, reaten, wraitten and many others.

Author comes from the Latin "to promote, increase." Authors, as we know, sell more books than writers do.

But authors crop up not only on promotional tours. An author also gives talks to young people about how to become an author. Youth looks upon him more or less expectantly, and if he were candid he would refer to his own school days and say, "All I ever wanted was for people not to look at me like I was a dip." But that wouldn't be authorial, and also he is afraid that "dip" may mean something completely different today. He advises plenty of writing, and reading.

An author reads. Not to himself, quietly; he has no time for that. To others, aloud. As it happens, literature is that which is lost aloud. The whole point of writing is to get something down in a voice that is better than the writer's own. When the writer tries to render this better voice *in* his own, the harmony isn't close. Sometimes too he may look up from such better-self abuse and make eye contact with someone in the audience. In its place, such contact may be all well and good. In literature . . . Say you are perusing away through *The Portrait of a Lady.* How would you like to turn a page and see, not the lady's, but Henry James's eye? In all its helpless ferocity. And do you think James would be at ease with yours?

An author also takes part in symposia. A symposium, even if all the panelists hate each other outright, is a more companionable affair than writing. However, a symposium poses a problem that the writer has devoted his life to avoiding: thinking of something worth saying while saying it.

A writer is loath to repeat himself. An author is bound to. Sometimes four times on different talk shows in one twelve-hour period in Philadelphia. An author is bound even to *quote* himself. With or without attribution. "It was I, I believe, who wrote . . ." It goes against the grain. (Of a writer.)

But authorship is not to be denied. Not even if you are Thomas Pynchon and stonewall all attempts to establish your actual existence. My own feeling is that Pynchon does not exist, and neither do the last five hundred pages of *Gravity's Rainbow*, but there is no question whatsoever that Thomas Pynchon is an author.

An author is a person who, if he or she is *not* a hermit, goes down to Memphis and is informed quite unlasciviously by a Friend of the Library, "You are my author for the afternoon."

An author is a person who is informed that he is to give a talk at a "Book and Author Dinner" and then a few days later is advised not to count on it, unless certain other authors cancel out, because the event's sponsors have realized that they invited too many Southern (or whatever the author's genus is) authors.

An author is a person who can never take innocent pleasure in visiting a bookstore again.

Say you go in and discover that there are no copies of your book on the shelves. You resent all the other books — I don't care if they are *Great Expectations, Life on the Mississippi* and the King James Bible — that are on the shelves. And then . . . Say you are Ewell Loblate, author of *Don't Try This at Home*.

You go to the counter and ask, "Do you have that book, uh, *Don't*, uh, *Try This . . . at Home*?" The clerk, who is listening to Black Sabbath through an earplug, looks blank.

"What's it on?" he says, after waiting to see whether you will leave.

21

"Oh, well, sort of . . . autobiogra . . . not *strictly*, but . . ."

By now there is no doubt in the clerk's mind that even if you won't leave, you should.

"Who's the author?" he inquires.

"Uh, I believe . . . something like . . ." Oh, the horror! "Lollib . . . Libl . . . uh, Loblate?"

The clerk makes an indifferent noise. "I'll call downstairs."

"Oh, you needn't . . ." But the machinery is in motion. After a long, long wait, as the clerk moves with understated sinuousness to some hellish cranial thrum and sells eleven copies of a book, on which high hopes are pinned, about weight loss through cats, here comes the conveyor belt, loudly, bearing a (the) copy of your book, blinking in the light.

Now, you don't want to *buy* your book. On an author's earnings, you can't afford it. On the other hand, you don't want to thumb through your book under the gaze of this person, this link to the reading public, and then say no, no thanks, you don't believe it is exactly what you had in mind.

But what you want most of all not to do is let the clerk catch sight of your picture on the jacket.

Which he does. "Hey!" he shouts, at last interested. "This looks like you!" More loudly. "This *you?*"

"Well . . . no. That is, I . . ."

"Hey, this *is* you! Hey! Here's an author! Asking for his own book! Hey, wouldn't they give you any? HEY!"

And all the shoppers in the store gather round and are joined from the street by several people who have never been in a bookstore before, and they all marvel and hoot and cry "Author!" and poke each other ("Says it's autobiographical!" cries the clerk), roll their eyes, press in to check the picture against your face for themselves, howl, then scatter, shaking their heads in disbelief. This happens to some authors several times a day.

Still, to author is to promote, to increase. To grow. One

develops a knack. I myself believe, in fact, that although I have had many years more experience at writing than at being an author, I am better at the latter. I think I would be quite good, for instance, at receiving prestigious awards. Any awards.

It may be that in time, taking one thing with the other, an author becomes inured. Develops a sense of himself as one of those bearded faces in Authors, the card game he played as a child. Pens one of those big two-page ads for the International Paper Company proving that today the printed word is more vital than ever.

I don't mean to suggest that I have myself made any real strides toward this reconciliation. But I did have an inkling of it once in Atlanta, on a radio call-in show. An elderly-sounding woman called in and said, "I saw you on the David Susskind program."

This, if I may say so without seeming churlish, is the kind of thing people say to authors. "I saw your book." "I saw your article in that magazine." "I saw you on something." Then they pause. If they were to go on and say, by some chance, "And it was [or you were] good," you could reply, "God bless you." But they do not go on and say anything. I tend to answer "God bless you" anyway and then regret it; but something in this call-in woman's tone led me to murmur noncommittally.

"And I want you to know," she went on, "that you gave a terrible account of the South."

"Ah, well," I countered lightly, knowing that similar things had been said of Jerry Lee Lewis, Walt Disney and Richard Wright.

"I knew your late daddy," she went on, "and I want you to know he'd be ashamed of you."

This did not sit well with me. Even authorial graciousness has its limits. "Did you know *your* daddy?" a writer, given time, would have riposted. The author, live on the air, huffed and gurgled.

"You mumbled," she continued, "your hair looked terrible, and you *slouched down in your seat.*"

With that she was gone. I sat there outraged. Forgot all my exiguously charted-out perceptions. Ventured, in response to the next caller, remarks that I realized, as they winged uneditably over the ether, were not only meaningless but, I regret to say, untrue.

Then came a call from another woman. A kind person. Who gave me the strength to author on.

"I saw you on David Susskind too," she said. "And I see all the authors that come on. And I want you to know," she said, "that you don't slouch any worse than Joyce Carol Oates."

BLUE YODEL 3

THREE YOUTHS

Three youths on subway. FIRST YOUTH, the shortest, says a girl has told him she wants him to leave her alone. He is inclined to leave her alone.

SECOND YOUTH: *Naw. That's what she* want *you to do.*

THIRD YOUTH: *Can't do that.*

SECOND YOUTH: *You do, she be the first one talking shit on you. "He a fag, I tole him to leave me alone; he leave me alone."*

THIRD YOUTH: *You can act like you leavin' her alone. But don't do it.*

The Lowdown on Southern Hospitality

COME on in! Busy? Me? No! Sit right down here in my favorite chair and keep me up all night and drink all my liquor. Can I run out and kill our last chicken and fry her up for you? No? Wouldn't take a minute. Are you *sure?* Oh, don't let the chicken hear you, she'll be so disappointed.

What *can* I do to make you comfortable?

You want me to tell you about Southern hospitality?

Well.

It is true that I live in the North, but am Southern. So I have a certain perspective. For one thing, living in the North enables me to retain the belief that there still is a South, as such.

In the past, to be sure, I have accepted invitations to speak in a Bogalusa, Louisiana, home on "Southern Hospitality: Is It All It's Cracked Up to Be?" and at an inn in Millinocket, Maine, on "Northern Hospitality: Why Isn't It Cracked Up to Be Anything?" I have engaged a descendant of General William Tecumseh Sherman in a widely reported debate, staged in a model Southern kitchen at the world's fair, on the question "Resolved: That to Be a Host in the North and a Guest in the South Is the Best of Both Worlds."

And yet I have a certain resistance to comparisons between Northern and Southern anything.

I do not say — although, in my capacity as host, I am *willing* to, if it will fulfill your expectations — that all regional generalizations appearing in Northern newspapers are wrong. Nor do I say that when a Northerner exclaims over Southern hospitality it is necessarily very much like Ronald Reagan's saying that if it weren't for women, men would still be carrying clubs.

I just don't want, myself, to pretend to be more of an expert than I am.

I am often asked: "What are Southern women like?" That is a question that many people feel entitled to an answer to. But I cannot speak with authority — not with authority as it is known in the South — about Southern women. I am acquainted with no more than two-thirds of them, and several of those I haven't seen in some time.

By the same token (it was Heraclitus, I believe, who said that you can enter the subway a thousand times, but never by the same token), I have not stayed in the great majority of homes and hotels, or patronized a majority of the stores and restaurants, in the South. Nor in the North, thank God. I have never gotten over the sight of whatever it was that was served to me as fried chicken one night in Akron.

"This is *fried* chicken?" I asked the waiter.

He looked at it. "I think so," he said.

I rest my case.

But that doesn't mean there is no such thing as Northern hospitality.

True, it is possible to meet with a less than heartwarming reception up North. I remember one Sunday morning in Cambridge, Massachusetts, I went to a cafeteria to get coffee and a donut before meeting a friend in business school.

I was greeted by a little machine that gave out tickets. I took a ticket, and ordered coffee and a donut from the woman behind the steam table, who was gazing with angst down into a vat of scrambled eggs. I was tempted to tell her I agreed that scrambled eggs should never be assembled in vat-sized proportions, but she seemed to be thinking about something even worse. Without speaking or even looking up, she served me and punched my ticket so as to show how

26

much I owed. I found a table, and after drinking my coffee, and eating my donut, and not bothering a soul, I presented the ticket to the woman at the cash register.

Everything seemed to be in order. I wasn't expecting anything more than a smooth transaction, but I was expecting that, a smooth transaction.

The woman at the cash register looked at my ticket, then raised her eyes as though in supplication. "Jaysus Murray and Jeosuph," she cried, pursing her lips unevenly like Humphrey Bogart. "Why do all you people come in on the weekends?"

That was nearly twenty years ago. To this day, I don't know what was wrong. I was too shaken to visit the business school, where they probably teach courses in putting the customer on the defensive.

But I wouldn't call that an example of Northern hospitality, exclusively. In Nashville, Tennessee, I cultivated a hamburger joint for weeks, ordering, with an iron will, the same thing every time. Finally I came in and said, "The usual."

"You mean 'the regular,'" the counter person, named Opaline, said.

"Well," I replied. I thought I meant "the usual." I thought *I* was the regular. But I didn't argue. "The regular, then," I said.

"In your case," she said, "what's that?"

Once I was driving through Kentucky, which is a border state. I stopped at a truck stop, at about 2 AM, for some coffee.

"Where's that kid sister of yours?" a skinny trucker was saying to one of the waitresses.

"Oh gone off. We don't know where," she said. "She's a wild kid, for nine."

"Hee-a-hee, I got a kick out of her," the skinny man said. "I'd say something and she'd come right back with something."

"She don't let you get nothing on her," the waitress said. "She's that much like Elizabeth."

Then a second waitress came over and said, perhaps in reference to Elizabeth, "You know she says she cleans out im sills evuh day, and Miz Clarkson come in here and said when im sills been cleaned out, and she said I done um this afternoon. And you know they was roaches in there that had died and was rotted. I said they sure do rot quick around here."

Well, I was put off a bit by such forthrightness about infestation, but I wanted to fall in with the camaraderie. Also, nobody had looked at me yet, and I needed coffee.

"No roaches in the coffee, are there?" I asked genially.

Immediately the waitress grew sullen. "No, at's just over'ere in im sills," she said. "You want some coffee?"

But I could tell she didn't care. There I was, at 2 AM, somewhere near a town called Sopping Gorge, in a diner where I wasn't wanted.

Still, Southern hospitality is an institution. Climate is a factor. In the South, people are more likely to be sitting out on the porch when folks show up. You can't pretend not to be at home, when there you are sitting on the porch. You can pretend to be dead, but then you can't fan yourself.

Rhetoric is another factor. The salesperson in Rich's Basement in Atlanta may give you just as glazed a look as the one in Filene's Basement in Boston, but the former is more likely to say, "These overalls are going to make your young one look cute as pea-turkey." Southerners derive energy from figures of speech, as plants do from photosynthesis.

I'll tell you something about Northerners, as a class: They don't think they are typical. A Southerner is too polite to tell them that they are. So they don't go out of their way to be. That is what's so typical about them.

Southerners get a charge out of being typical. If a Northern visitor makes it clear to Southerners that he thinks it would be typical of them to rustle up a big, piping hot meal of hushpuppies and blackstrap, Southerners will do that, even if they were planning to have just a little salad that night.

Then the visitor will ask how to eat hushpuppies and blackstrap. If a Southerner were to go up North and ask how, or why, he was supposed to eat sushi, Northerners would snicker. But Southerners don't even let on to a Northerner that he is being typical when he asks how you eat hushpuppies and blackstrap.

The strictly accurate answer is that nobody in his or her right mind eats these two things, together, in any way at all. But that isn't a sociable answer. So Southerners may say, "First you pour your plate full of the molasses, and then you crumble your hushpuppies up in it, and then you take the *back* of your spoon, and . . ." Southerners will say things like that just to see whether it is still true that Northerners will believe anything. About the South.

Northerners, too, will explain things to visitors. It is a misconception that nobody in New York City, for instance, will offer you any guidance on the street. If you allow your pace to lag for a moment, longtime residents will assume you're from out of town (which as far as they are concerned could be Delaware or Namibia), and will come running up to you asking, triumphantly, "Are you lost?" Then they will start giving you directions. These directions are usually wrong (although you can't count on it), but they enable longtime residents to feel that they are *not* lost.

That is one kind of distinctive Northern hospitality. Another kind is when you walk into a dry cleaner's for the thirtieth time and the proprietor, recognizing you at last, says, "You again!" If you are willing to accept that he is never going to welcome you, then you're welcome.

The advantage of this form of Northern hospitality is that

it works irritation right into the equation, up front. Let's face it, people irritate each other. Especially hosts and guests.

The truth is, irritation is involved in Southern hospitality too. Say you run into a Southerner where you live in the North. And you take a thorn out of his paw or something and he declares, "I want you to come visit us! And I want you to sleep in my bed! Me and Momma will take the cot! And bring your whole family!"

"Yes, do come," says the Southern wife. "We would *love* it."

"And I want you to hold my little baby daughter on your lap!" her husband cries. "And Momma will cook up a whole lot of groceries and we'll all eat ourselves half to death!"

And sure enough, you show up. And the Southerners swing wide the portal and blink a little, and then recognize you and start hollering: "You came! Hallelujah! Sit down here! How long can you stay? Oh, no, you got to stay longer than a week, it'll take that long just to eat the old milk cow. Junior, run out back and kill the old milk cow. Milk her first.

"Here, let us carry all your bags — oh, isn't this a nice trunk — upstairs and . . ."

You are a little disappointed to note that there is no verandah.

"Oh, we lost our verandah in the Waw. Which Waw? Why the Waw with *you* all. But that's all right."

And you are prevailed upon to stay a *couple* of weeks, and you yield to the Southerners' insistence that you eat three huge meals a day and several snacks — and finally you override the Southerners' pleas that you stay around till the scuppernongs get ripe, and they say, "Well, I guess if you got your heart set on leaving us," in a put-out tone of voice, and they pack up a big lunch of pecan pie and collard greens for you to eat on the way home, and after you go through about an hour and a half of waving, and repeating that you really do have to go, and promising to come back, soon, and to bring more of your relatives next time, you go on back North.

And the Southerners close their door. And they slump back up against it. And they look at each other wide-eyed. And they say, shaking their heads over the simplemindedness of Yankees, *"They came!"*

"And like to never left!"

"And ate us out of house and home!"

Nothing — not even the sight of people eating hushpuppies mushed up in blackstrap molasses — is sweeter than mounting irritation prolongedly held close to the bosom.

BLUE YODEL 4

ROGER

I don't understand guys who say they're feminists. That's like the time Hubert Humphrey, running for President, told a black audience that he was a soul brother.

And say you fall in love with somebody and it turns out she's not a feminist. It happens. You've kind of painted yourself into a corner now, haven't you? What are you going to say — you've always believed in feminism but you'll give it up for her? How's she going to take that?

Another thing. Do not be more Catholic than the Pope. You know what I'm saying?

High-heel shoes. The other night I'm watching Miss America. Cheryl walks in and says, "That's disgusting. Women parading around in bathing suits and heels!"

"You're right," I say. "If there was a show on television, of men walking around in bathing suits and high heels, I'd think it was disgusting. And I think this is disgusting. In

31

fact, high-heel shoes to begin with! Talk about barbarous practices! They're like foot binding."

"Mm," she says, and I should've quit then.

"I'll tell you the whole point of high-heel shoes," I say. "It's so Madeleine Carroll can't run fast and Robert Donat has to keep reaching back and helping her along when they're fleeing the authorities. Without high-heel shoes, Madeleine Carroll can probably beat Robert Donat by half a dozen strides over a hundred yards, and the system can't have that!"

"Mm," she says, and I sure should've quit then.

"But you know what?" I say. "I don't think men like high-heel shoes on women. Particularly. I don't think men — I mean individual husbands and things — make women wear 'em. If every woman in the world started wearing penny-loafers, I don't think it would bother men. Men like women with as few shoes on as possible. Granted, hookers wear high heels. But I think hookers dress for other hookers. I'll tell you another thing — women having to pierce their ears. I don't think men get excited over earrings on women either. And when I see Chrissie Evert playing tennis in earrings . . ."

I notice Cheryl is silent.

"Don't you think?" I say. "About high heels," I say. "I mean, if you like high heels, it's fine. It just . . . seems like they're . . . You see what I mean?"

I notice Cheryl is still silent.

"I was just . . . ," I say. "I mean . . . Make your legs look good and all, I guess. But your legs look good anyway. Great anyway. And don't high heels kind of bunch up your — women's. People's. Calves? I don't know. Maybe it's just . . . Taller of course too, but men don't . . . And, heh-heh, your butt too, but . . . You see what I mean?"

"Why is it so important to you?" she snaps.

On Hats

CLOTHES are not my strong suit, but I do know this: Public hanging ended in England because of the hat.

According to Richard D. Altick, in *Victorian Studies in Scarlet*, a German named Müller murdered an elderly man on a North London Railway train in 1864 and was convicted because he accidentally exchanged hats with the victim after a struggle. His own hat was found in the compartment, and he was presently discovered wearing the victim's — only with the crown cut down so as to eliminate the victim's name on the inside. Forthwith there sprang up a stylish hat, like a topper only half as tall, called the Müller cut-down. The crowd that gathered during the night before Müller's hanging was unruly. Several well-dressed congregants were bonneted — that is, someone sneaked up from behind and pulled their hats down over their faces — garroted, and robbed. Parliament was at last provoked to forbid public executions.

The hat. Our most resonant garment. According to *Folk Beliefs of the Southern Negro*, by Newbell Niles Puckett, American slaves (who had to believe in something other than America) believed that if you put on another person's hat you'll get a headache unless you blow into the hat first; that it is bad luck to put your hat on inside out; that the bad luck promised by a rabbit's crossing the road ahead of you may be averted by putting your hat on backward; that if you desire eggs to hatch into roosters you should carry them to the nest in a man's hat; that a group of people was once crossing a field at noon when they suddenly saw a whole house coming after them, which passed so close that it knocked off their hats, and neither hats nor house was seen again; that if you eat with your hat on you will not get enough.

And yet it seems to me that people these days wear hats lightly. People have somehow gotten hold of the notion that a hat is a fun topping. Nothing in this world makes a person who is not a cowboy look less like a cowboy than wearing a cowboy hat, and yet we have recently passed through a period when every third nonpunk person in New York and Los Angeles was in for the full ten gallons.

Hey! You can't just walk around *wearing a cowboy hat.* I don't walk around wearing one, and I have herded cows. Somehow years ago I lost the tan felt cowboy hat I got (with the card inside that says "Like Hell It's Yours") at the White Front Store in Fort Worth. I wore it on working visits to a Texas cattle ranch to which I was then related by marriage. That hat and I were rained on twice, and the trained eye could discern traces of horse slobber on its brim and a touch of cow paddy (it can happen) on its crown. That hat fit me so well that — well, I'll tell you how well it fit me.

One evening a bunch of us were in the back of a pickup truck, hurtling through the night toward a mudhole to pull out a mired heifer. It was too dark for abandoned driving, but the driver, Herman Posey, got caught up in the holiday spirit pervading us visitors, and before we knew it he had us jouncing and plummeting, off the ground more than on it, over creek bed, armadillo, and cactus.

Bob Crittendon, the foreman, was with us in the back. He weighed a good deal more than two hundred pounds and didn't find any charm in being jounced. He was busy yelling, "*Herman, damn you, slow down!*"

And yet he took the time to mention, "Old Roy's the only one don't have to hold on to his hat."

And. Yet. I wouldn't wear that hat around town.

When I'm around town I don't want to be always *backing*

up a hat. You might think it would back up that hat for me to tell that story about what Bob Crittendon said. But it wouldn't be the same as hearing Bob say it. To back up a cowboy hat you have to think of a remark of your own, like the one a man I know named Jimmy Crafton, in Nashville, thought of when a man picked his cowboy hat up off a bar and tried it on.

Crafton gave him a look.

The man thought better of what he had done, and apologized.

"That's all right," said Crafton. "That's why I wear a fifty-dollar hat. If it was a two-hundred-dollar hat," he explained, "I'da had to kill you."

I'll say another thing. Nobody ought to wear a Greek fisherman's cap who doesn't meet two qualifications:

1. He is Greek.
2. He is a fisherman.

What I am getting at is, a hat ought not to be on a head for a whim. Yeats once said that when a poem is finished it "comes right with a click like a closing box." That's what a hat ought to do for a person. Quite often today, though the person may think it does, it doesn't.

I like to wear a hat around home and driving, because it obviates hair combing and it helps keep the bugs off. (There is no hat that keeps you warm in serious winter. If they ever invented a hat that kept your ears and neck warm it would be a hood and it might as well be attached to your coat.) What I usually wear is some kind of billed, adjustable cap.

And these days those caps all, just about, have something written on them. I stay away from the ones that say "I'm a Real Dilly," or "Texas Turkey" (with a picture of an armadillo). For some time I wore one that said "Shakespeare" for Shakespeare brand fishing equipment, because those folks make good fishing equipment and I wasn't averse to paying indirect tribute to the author of *King Lear*. And I had been given that hat free. And it fit my head. You'd be surprised how many people walk around in hats that don't fit their heads, and also how many "One Size Fits All" adjustable hats don't fit all. But that one fit me. But I left it hanging in a Howard Johnson's on the interstate and couldn't go back for it.

Then for a while I had a cap that said "MF," for Massey-Ferguson farm and industrial equipment, and that cap brought home to me that a hat is language.

I was wearing that cap out on the road and one of my tires went flat and wouldn't hold air longer than twenty miles and nobody could seem to patch it, and I didn't have a spare. I had to go to a place that sold tires, and the man was just closing up, but he was kind enough to turn his lights back on and chain his dog back up and sell me a tire and put it on.

And he took my cap at face value. Assumed I was a Massey-Ferguson representative. Plunged into a series of questions about what kind of tractor would be best for working the little piece of land he had at home, and could I maybe get him some kind of deal on one.

And I had to tell him I didn't represent Massey-Ferguson. And he took it the wrong way. Here he was staying open late to help me out, and either I was fraudulent or else I didn't want to admit that I could get him a deal. He kept shooting looks over at my cap (so did his dog) while he worked, and I thought he was going to tell me to take it off. And I could see how he felt. But I didn't want to think that I was going to let somebody tell me to take my *hat* off, you know. I got out of there all right, except I think he charged me an extra ten dollars for my cap.

Then a couple of weeks later I had the same cap on and a friend from New York looked at it and said, "Oh, a football coach's cap."

"A what?" I said.

"A football coach's cap," she said. "That's what you call them. They're very big now in the gay community."

Now, a gay person has every bit as much right to wear a Massey-Ferguson cap as I have; more right if he's a Massey-Ferguson representative. Or owns a tractor that the cap came with. But I didn't like it that my cap all of a sudden had a term for it, among the fashion-conscious.

But that's the way a hat is, it's like a word: you have to keep up with all its shifting connotations if you're going to employ it. And you have to avoid assuming too quickly that you do know them. There is a telling hat scene in the movie *Deliverance*. The city guys stop at a gas station up in the hills. Bobby, the chubby character played by Ned Beatty, espies a toothless-looking, shuffling mountain man with an old felt hat pulled down over his ears. "Hey, we got a live one here," Bobby says. The man begins to fill their tank. "I love the way you wear that hat," Bobby tells him. The man takes off the hat, turns it around in his hands, looks at it, jams it back on his head.

"Mister," he says, "you don't know *nuthin'*."

If you saw the movie, you remember what happens to Bobby.

BLUE YODEL 5

VINNIE AND DOM

VINNIE: . . . *things these days. My mother wants to know why I won't let her ride the bus to St. Mary the Virgin. I say, "Because you got bit in the back of the neck, Ma." Guy on the bus bit my mother in the back of the neck! I hit the guy . . . I found the guy. I hit the guy . . .*

DOM: *Guys like that shouldn't be hit. Guys like that, you should kill 'em.*

VINNIE: *I beat the shit out of the guy.*

DOM: *Guys like that, you shouldn't beat the shit out of them. You should kill guys like that.*

VINNIE: *She says she wishes she didn't tell me. I say, "Ma, you told me. Just go to St. Francis's up the block here." She says but at St. Mary the Virgin the stations of the cross are prettier. I say, "Ma, our Savior didn't tell us, seek out a place with pretty stations of the cross to go to mass." She says she don't understand. I say, "Ma, you have to listen to me now. If you don't understand, I can't tell you. Don't take the bus no more."*

DOM: *Guys like that, you ought to kill 'em.*

VINNIE: *What does she want me to say? "You want a son that went to the penitentiary for murder and had to fight off six-foot-six black bodybuilder fruits with a sharpened bedspring for the rest of his life because you got to ride the bus to see the prettier stations of the cross at St. Mary the Virgin?"?*

DOM: *Just kill 'em. That's all.*

Women in the Locker Room!

I'LL TELL you who — if he were with us in this hour — would be the ideal dressing-room reporter.

Undrape! you are not guilty to me, nor stale nor discarded,
I see through the broadcloth and gingham whether or no,
And am around, tenacious, acquisitive, tireless, and cannot
*   be shaken away.*

Walt Whitman. If you read it right, "Song of Myself" is all about sportswriting.

Blacksmiths with grimed and hairy chests environ the anvil,

Each has his main-sledge, they are all out, there is a great
   heat in the fire.

From the cinder-strew'd threshold I follow their move-
   ments,
The lithe sheer of their waists plays even with their massive
   arms,
Overhand the hammers swing, overhand so slow, overhand
   so sure,
They do not hasten, each man hits in his place.

Wouldn't Walt be hell rhapsodizing on batting practice?
His sensitivities are masculine enough, so to speak, that he
can really get into hammering, and feminine enough, so to
speak, that he can be turned on by men's waists. We don't
have any Whitmans among the locker-room-invading press
today, but we do have women.

These women face the same deadlines and inside-flavor
requirements that men reporters do. So why should they be
forced to wait outside, in the hall or in a special interview
room, while their male competitors walk right in and grill
the players in the act of taking their pants off one leg at a
time? It is not uncommon today to see Lois Lane in the
phone booth with supermen of nearly every team sport —
partly because of a lawsuit filed against Major League Baseball in 1977 by Melissa Ludtke and her then employer,
Sports Illustrated.

"If those broads don't watch it, they're going to get us all
thrown out," a prominent male scribe exclaimed at the
time.

"Bowie Kuhn really screwed up," Ludtke said of the
baseball commissioner, whose denial of her application
for World Series locker-room credentials led to her sex-
discrimination suit. "He opened up a can of worms across
the board. He could have worked something out. But now if
we win, there won't be any way a woman can be kept out by
any club down to the high-school level, really, which is

ridiculous." Barbara Walters surrounded by slack-jawed naked Murfreesboro Blue Devils — she's trying to get them to be serious, they're popping her with towels . . . That has not yet come to pass, alas.

A couple of years ago, I was sitting next to Stephanie Salter, who used to cover sports for the *San Francisco Examiner*, when she was ejected — "We'll call a cop!" — from the New York Baseball Writers' annual dinner for not being a stag. Because I would generally rather eat with a friend of mine who has been tossed out of somewhere than with someone who has done the tossing, I walked out with her; but I hated missing Casey Stengel's postdinner remarks.

The previous year, Stengel had laid down an ageless boyish sports guideline when he said of one of his stauncher ex-players, "When it came time to piss in the road, he pissed harder than anybody." It was to preserve speakers' freedom to say such things, I suppose, that women were excluded. I doubt that Stengel, then around eighty and as full of strange music as *Finnegans Wake*, would have been inhibited by a woman's presence, or by anything short of a fire bomb, but there does seem to be an issue there somewhere. Men may suspect that a woman will regard pissing hard in the road as something quaintly obstreperous, something that only a man who "has to prove himself" would care about. My wife says she doesn't think women feel this way. My wife has been in the dressing room of the Pittsburgh Pirates. I have told her I don't want to hear about it.

But colleges have coed dorms, don't they? Olympic athletes have to take sex tests, don't they? And at least one World Team Tennis team was known to make do with a single dressing room for its men and women players. Strictly speaking, a dressing room with self-respecting men reporters in it is not a stag affair anyway, because self-respecting reporters are going to report some of the proceedings to readers, including women. Most of the really fun stuff that goes on in dressing rooms, like running nude and landing seated in a teammate's birthday cake, goes on when reporters of all sexes are absent.

I can't claim to have felt like a woman in a men's dressing room, but I have been made to feel rather ... chirpy, and like a second-class citizen, by male players who didn't like sharing their scene with Clark Kent. An interviewee may have no towel around his waist yet still have one around his mind. On the other hand, the first time I brought my young son into the locker room of the Pittsburgh Steelers, we were received like two of the boys (somebody even threw a little piece of soap at us), and it was the zenith of my credibility as a father.

Which reminds me: Former Steeler Bruce Van Dyke's son was a toddler when Van Dyke brought him into the dressing room for the first time. Van Dyke looked away for a moment, and when he turned back, the lad had gotten so thoroughly into the spirit of the place that he was naked.

"People won't believe that nakedness is not the problem," said Ludtke, after having been into basketball dressing rooms as well as baseball clubhouses. Like the other women reporters who first penetrated these sancta, she was interviewed in newspapers and on the radio all over the country. "I was on a call-in show in Pittsburgh for an hour," she said, "and all anybody wanted to talk about was nakedness. Every subject would be turned around to nakedness. There were grandmothers worried about their grandsons facing this onslaught of women, and there were other women who just didn't think it was right. Before I went into this business, I wouldn't have seen the necessity of it either. But the players can use a towel if they want to. And when you're interviewing somebody, it's eye-to-eye and mouth-to-notebook-and-pen sort of contact. I don't just sit there *looking.*"

The dressing rooms that admit women reporters have done so only after the players have voted their approval, and for the most part, players seem to have adjusted to the onslaught pretty well, though with ethnic differences. Generally, young black players have been the least self-conscious, I am told. Lawrie Mifflin, who covered hockey and soccer for the *New York Daily News*, told me there is a New York Cosmo from Italy who always wears a bathrobe in the clubhouse, women or no. Everybody does in Italian clubhouses.

Jane Gross of the *New York Times*, a pioneer woman in NBA dressing rooms, has written about finding in the locker room "a kind of caring for each other you don't see often in groups of women."

"The dressing room is a place where I don't feel I belong," said Salter, speaking more as a press person than as a woman, "but the players have gotten used to me. In fact, sometimes they talk to me because it's harder to tell a woman to go away." Kareem Abdul-Jabbar did ask her to please get her knee off his stool, but that could have happened to Grantland Rice (assuming he was limber enough to reach Jabbar's stool with his knee). Another superstar embarrassed Salter the same way he would any male reporter who pinned him down. "He was complaining about 'not being a part of the offense.'" she said, "and I asked him if he was saying that he was pissed off because his teammates weren't getting him the ball. He started yelling in front of everybody, 'That's exactly the kind of question — that's exactly what the press gets wrong!' And then he flounced off to the john. Later I sat down with him and got him to explain what he meant. Essentially, it was that he was pissed off because his teammates weren't getting him the ball."

Lawrie Mifflin said she felt quite comfortable in locker rooms because she grew up in them, as an interscholastic field-hockey player. "In my school the cheerleaders were the strange ones, who couldn't make the team," she said. She added that she was close to her brothers and belonged to the first coeducational class at Yale — as did the *New York Times*'s Robin Herman at Princeton.

"The first time I walked into a dressing room," said Herman, "there were about fifty men in suits in the middle of the room, and then the athletes undressing in a ring around them. I thought, 'I'll just melt into this group of clothed people . . .' Of course it didn't work out that way. Cameras started flashing, and people were asking *me* questions. It *is* a strange setting. Where else in life do people talk to people while they're dressing? Unless it's a husband or a wife or your children. Even your parents don't talk to you while you're dressing. You notice all kinds of things in the dressing room. Like people who put on their shoes and socks before their undershirt. Things you don't really want to know." But she and Mifflin were for a while the only reporters traveling with the New York Rangers, and Herman said she eventually became convinced the players had "forgotten we're women."

The only way her exposure to dressing rooms had affected her feelings toward men, Herman said, was that "I'm really spoiled now in favor of men who take care of their bodies. I don't think I could go out with a skinny guy who gets sand kicked in his face." Some women reporters rule out romance with players, and some don't. One says players never ask her out until after they've left the dressing room. "I guess undressed is a very vulnerable state to be rejected in. I could say, 'Why would I go out with you? Look at you!' "

After all, these reporters are women, and their slants are somewhat different from men's. Maybe they will dispel some of the stale cigar smoke that suffuses the sportswriting profession. Not that all such smoke should go, from the press box or from the stands, but it is refreshing to hear a sportswriter say that a player "flounced" or that jockeys "just chattered and chattered until they got on their horses and rode off," as Salter did, or that the New York Islanders "are still kind of skittish," as Herman did. It is also interesting, though odd, to hear a woman reporter say that a certain veteran player "is beginning to look like a saggy old woman."

She was not going to put that in the paper. But one reason why anybody who covers a team should have access to the dressing room is that the bodies are such a big part of the story.

"Sure, it's interesting, to look at their chests and shoulders," said Mifflin. "But if I say that, then people will say, 'See, they claim it's not sexual, but she's been looking at their bodies!'"

"I have no apologies to make," said Herman. "I know why I'm looking and what I'm looking for. Seeing the way they're built helps you understand the way they play. But I feel like I'm treading on dangerous ground now, talking about it."

Exactly the kind of ground Walt Whitman liked. Let us have wide, nonprurient male and female eyes in the dressing room, because significant bodies ought to be witnessed. The most remarkable one I ever saw was Satchel Paige's. His huge feet were completely archless, spread across the floor, with all the toes bent sharply to the right for some reason, and his lower legs were heavily scarred and as straight as Popeye's upper arms. And yet dressed, as he said himself, he looked "like a young doctor."

I like to see players in the flesh because I never cease to entertain, as a point of reference, the eternal sportswriter's question: "Why is this guy getting paid to play ball and not me?" I have seen players whose bodies immediately implied every foot-pound their games must require, which is more oomph than I can imagine commanding. I have seen a *few* players whose bodies looked less prepossessing than mine. Then there are the scars and bent limbs.

So, you're going to ask next, should men reporters be allowed in women's locker rooms? Well, I'm going to reply in a measured tone, we generally don't need to yet, because those women's sports, such as tennis, that are heavily reported are not really team sports, and it's possible to catch all the principals before they go off to dress. Women's basketball, however, thanks to recent strides toward equality in funding of women's intercollegiate sports, has been attracting more and more deadline-pressure coverage. Male reporters have, in fact, been in women's basketball locker rooms after games already, but the players have kept their uniforms on until the press left. I'm told it looks strange, a dressing room full of people with no dressing going on. Presumably there would be too much ogling if a lot of male scribes were to barge into a functioning sanctum of women. But women can wear towels too, and a band of athletes has a corporate air that discourages even optical barging. Wouldn't any sincere nonsexist student of sport take a respectful interest in what a woman strong-forward's chest and shoulders look like? I know Walt Whitman would have — he who asked all the crucial sportswriting questions:

Who goes there? hankering, gross, mystical, nude;
How is it I extract strength from the beef I eat?

What is a man anyhow? what am I? what are you?

BLUE YODEL 6

MURRAY

The big thing is, make sure men keep ahold of the movie cameras.
Women are the elementary and high-school teachers. (Except for coaches, and they only teach Civics, and after the first five minutes of the period they go off to watch films of next week's opponent while the class copies the principles

of bicameralism and separation of powers off the board.)
Because the pay is shitty, women mold kids' minds. Therein
lies tyranny, if it ever goes unchecked.

So men have to hold on to the movie cameras. Women
may become governors, policemen, generals, and bank offi-
cials in charge of denying people loans. Fine. Movie cameras
are the eye of the beholder.

Movie cameras tell us what is a wonder to behold. As
long as women feel, deep down inside, that they are the ones
who are wonders to behold when beheld in the right light in
flimsy negligees, they will continue to hug each other, wear
makeup, buy Gothic novels, go to the restroom in pairs, and
leave the seizing of territory to others.

Granted, there are naked men in movies now. The cam-
era focuses in on Richard Gere's hiney. Okay. I'm not deny-
ing that Richard Gere's hiney constitutes a threat. I think
we all recognize this: If it ever gets to where all men's hineys
are seen in the light of Richard Gere's, it is the end of civili-
zation as we know it. The whole point of being the gender in
power is that you don't have to be shapely to be attractive.
Power that worries about whether its hiney is beautiful is
not power. Those in power cover their ass. Except for those
in raw or naked power, who show it — but in an insulting
way.

However. The movie camera is focusing in on Richard
Gere's hiney. But the camera is being handled by a person
who is thinking, "Okay. Here it is. For whoever is in-
terested. Seen enough? Great."

Now the movie camera focuses in on a sultry new tempt-
ress's hiney. The camera is in the hands of a person who is
thinking, "Holy, jumping . . . Maybe she'll turn around!
Maybe she'll turn around!"

But don't tell women that.

Because then you also have to try to tell them that a life
of seizing territory is no bargain. And they don't want to
hear it.

46

Hey, somebody's got to seize it. And hold it and pay for redecorating it and keep the Communists off it. So women can bitch about there's not good enough shopping on it, not enough opportunities for women on it, you didn't seize enough of it yet, it's not an ideal place to raise children.

Which is fine. If I'm a woman, that's what I bitch about too. But before you can bitch about it, somebody's got to seize it. And try getting a woman to listen to you bitch about being saddled with the territorial imperative.

Territory used to be what American men could light out for. Right? To get away from wives, aunts, and teachers. Now every piece of territory — in the world — somebody owns it, and somebody else is claiming it. Strip miners, the PLO, followers of the guru Bugwug, Mobil, Shiites, and the peacekeeping forces — all shoving each other on and off territory.

There's nothing left to light out for. Space? Space? The Pentagon, the Kremlin, and Big Science already own space. By the time anybody develops a one-seater space coupe that a man can go off into space on his own in, there won't be any room left in space. It'll all be zoned.

You know what computer people call the space on the teeny tiny weeny microchip where they place the little hyper-mini doodads or conductors or circuits? They call it "real estate." Try lighting out for territory like that.

The only thing left to light out for is sultry new temptresses. On the screen. We don't have to seize, own, or maintain 'em. They are wonders to behold. To disappear into. As long as we've got the cameras.

He Took the Guilt
out of the Blues

I HAVE Elvis's last afternoon paper. Or what would have been, if he had lived into the evening of August 16, 1977. I was in Nashville that day. When somebody brought the news into the greasy spoon where I was sitting, the juke-box — I swear — had just finished playing Elvis's latest hit, "Way Down."

ELVIS THE PELVIS, ELVIS LIVES, ELVIS'S EVILS, ELVIS IS VILE, ELVIS'S VEILS (oddly, Elvis disliked Levi's — too close to poverty britches, I guess) all seemed to be in the nature of things, but ELVIS DEAD was a jolt. I flew to Memphis. "What's that?" I asked Fred Stoll, Elvis's gatekeeper, at Graceland late that night. "That's Elvis's last *Press-Scimitar*," said Stoll. So I stole it. It still had the rubber band on, until I opened it while writing this piece and the dried-out rubber snapped.

Elvis in his coffin was fat, glowering, and surrounded by similar-looking but vertical heavies who pushed us viewers along. Reportedly, Elvis had died "straining at the stool" while reading a book about the discovery of Christ's skele-ton. You couldn't disprove it by looking at him. ELVIS DEAD, all right. But not at peace. He looked like he wanted to make another big leap, but couldn't. He didn't look cool.

Neither did the thousands of people who gathered at the gates of Graceland. People fainted left and right, from the heat, the crowding, and the historical moment. And because if you fainted, you got carried onto the grounds.

"He was really a good man," said a stringy woman wear-ing off-brand jeans and a halter top revealing a midriff with two moles and a fresh abrasion. "To achieve superstardom

48

at that age and keep his basic Christian qualities. I don't see how he did it. I don't really know."

"He coulda lived another no telling how long," said a fat woman in lemon-lime shorts. "But he just kinda gave himself to the people."

A mother in her late thirties kept edging herself and her little girl, about four, toward the Graceland gate. The girl was crying. An altercation developed in front of them. I don't think anyone could tell what the roots of the disturbance were, but the police moved in and collared a black man. He yelled. He'd been waiting so long. One cop cuffed the man's hands behind his back and thrust a nightstick between the man's legs. Another cop grabbed the other end of the stick and they carried the man away like that, riding him out of Elvis Nation on a rail. The man made a strangled noise. The mother took the occasion to push her daughter, who was screaming now, beyond the barricades and through the gate and into the line, past banks of floral displays (and Styrofoam crosses and artificial roses and gilded plastic cardinals or blue jays), to see the dead man.

You might like Ray and Chuck and Jerry Lee better, and also Little Richard, but I doubt you would fly to see them, God forbid, in their coffins. Whatever else you think about Elvis, he was epochal.

When I was in the eighth grade, 1954, I got wind of "Annie Had a Baby" ("cain' wuck no mo") and heard reports of black music shows in Atlanta from fellow adolescents more advanced than I who would wink at each other and repeat the catchphrase "hunchin' and a-jackin'." I don't know what song that was from, but it made more of an impression on me than Elvis Presley did. Of course, when Elvis came, he was on "The Ed Sullivan Show." You didn't have to be cool to know about Elvis. "We've lost the most popular man that ever walked on this planet since Christ was here himself," said Carl Perkins when Elvis died.

The summer after eighth grade, I went to a party at the house of my Babe Ruth League coach, a wizened and taciturn mill-worker whom you would not expect to figure in a pelvic revolution. But the coach's boys had organized the party, and one of Elvis's first singles was playing. My coach's equally wizened but more voluble elder son came up and asked me, earnestly, "Do you think Elvis has got it?"

"Yes," I said. Though I was no authority. This was my first rock-criticism conversation — one of the few, in fact, that I have had over the years — and my soundest one. Elvis had managed to make music that hunched and jacked and yet could be heard in one's baseball coach's home. It didn't grab and unsettle me like "Annie Had a Baby," or like Ray Charles or Chuck Berry or Jerry Lee Lewis, and it still doesn't. But it had it. And it made it mellifluous.

There is a wonderful Alice Walker short story, "Nineteen Fifty-Five," about a black blues singer like Big Mama Thornton, who did the first version of "Hound Dog," and a white muddled megarocker like the late Elvis. The Elvis character is guiltily beholden to her, and she says things like, "It don't matter, Son." At the end of the story it comes over the TV that the Elvis character is dead. The Big Mama character doesn't want to watch his fans grieve. "They was crying and crying and didn't know what they was crying for. One day this is going to be a pitiful country, I thought."

And here's what Chuck Berry said when asked on TV right after Elvis's death what Elvis would be remembered for: "Oh boop, boop, boop; shake your leg; fabulous teen music; the fifties; his movies."

But Elvis didn't just siphon off some negritude and slick it up. ("Hound Dog" was written by Leiber and Stoller, who added to the black culture they appropriated and didn't try to appropriate any more than they could carry.) His h-and-j was fired by poor-white disrepressed defiance, and to it he added mooniness, juvenility, niceness, hope, fuzz, hype, and androgyny. Rock 'n' roll.

Where Janis Joplin began by trying to sing the blues as unseasoned homely-white-girl hysteria, Elvis's sudden rockabilly was fresh and centripetal. He took the guilt out of the blues, says Greil Marcus. That is like taking the grit out of the beach or the smell out of the collards, but Elvis did it. It got people — white people I guess I mostly mean, but aren't white people Americans too? — wiggling. The next thing you knew, there was a Youth Culture, which I think we may assume Elvis did not dream of in 1954. I know I didn't.

The Youth Culture took wiggling for granted, and Mick Jagger's pelvis was to Elvis's as a Cuisinart is to a mortar and pestle. But Elvis was an old redneck boy who loved gospel and drove a truck. He might just about as well have grown up to be Jerry Falwell. For a boy with Elvis's background to move the way he did suddenly proved something, as in 1929 when the *rich* started bailing out. The jump from not shaking that thing at all to shaking it was bigger than the segue from shaking it to undulation. It was Elvis, you could say with some justice, who goosed mainstream America into that jump.

Elvis didn't fit into the Youth Culture. He ballooned — began to wear a girdle, as decent girls did before he came along. He became a martyr: to the new level of profligate absurd glamour-power he established, and to his own abiding adolescence. After his death, when Big Mama Thornton was asked how she felt about having made a hundred dollars or so from "Hound Dog" compared with Elvis's millions, she said, "I'm still here to *spend* my hundred dollars."

Though ever a (naughty) mama's boy, Elvis sprang beyond Big Mama; special effects outjump flesh and blood every time. Even before the pill, Elvis seemed to obviate the primacy of Jack-hunch-Annie-and-knock-her-up. Boy fans tended to approach him more reservedly than did the girls, to whom he seemed to be saying — *trustworthily* — that he could do you without getting you in trouble, and vice versa.

"Hound Dog" made grim traditional sense as a woman's

song about a trifling man. Elvis's version was vaguely raunchy, mostly adorable. How could there be any downside to a man who looked both wholesome and sultry, a man whose sensual lips sang "Don't be cruel, to a heart that's true"? "Sex is dynamite," generations of American mothers had been telling their daughters, and by *dynamite* they didn't mean "fabulous." They meant "ruination." Elvis probably would have said, "Yes'm, I know," to every one of those mothers, and yet he lit that dynamite and went pop. And grinned. Elvis's grin, like FDR's, was historic. It got young people on the road to concluding that they had nothing to feel guilty about but guilt itself, that parents were wrong about sex and probably about everything else, that the System (parents), not the heart, was where all the shadows lay.

Over the long haul Elvis was more of a crooner than a rocker. But he was a frontiersman. Ray and Chuck and Jerry Lee remained "cut-the-cards, you-*know*-what-I'm-carrying" guys, who are never likely to be accused, as Elvis was in a recent, cankered biography by Albert Goldman, of preferring that girls leave their panties on. The other night I watched a tape of Elvis's 1968 comeback TV concert. He looked like Martin Sheen, Jack Palance, Katy Jurado, Sal Mineo, Ann-Margret (the mouth), and a touch of Grady Sutton. He was pretty, tough, vaunting, shy, dumb, wily, boring, startling, saturnine, and mercurial. Elvis wasn't just heteroerotic; he was close to Norman O. Brown's polymorphous perverse.

Rock 'n' roll evolved in that direction. (I wonder what Elvis made of David Bowie.) And so did American culture until about the time Elvis died. Now there's a different trend. Ronald Reagan, George Shultz, Jesse Helms, George Will, and Frank Sinatra show few traces of the rock revolution. The culture seems to be doubling back, looking for something it dropped. Do you know what my adolescent kids are listening to? Besides Dire Straits' "Industrial Disease"? They are listening to a group called Stray Cats, who play rockabilly.

But they are listening to it with looser hips than I did.

BLUE YODEL 7
RALEIGH

Women's case rests on two assumptions: one, that seated activity is normal, and two, that standing activity is aberrant.

In defense of these assumptions, women point out that of the two forms of activity, which we will call number one and number two, everyone performs number two seated. Seated activity, then, is part of everyone's experience. And seated activity requires that the seat be down. Therefore, women argue, the seat should always be left down for the next person.

For decades men have tried to get number two thrown out, on the grounds that it is the less frequent activity and should not carry as much weight as number one; that it confuses the issue, which should be confined to number one. Men have never been successful.

So men's argument is as follows: If women are injured by finding that the seat has been left up, then why are men not injured by finding that the seat has been left down?

Women respond that the way in which women discover that the seat has been left up — i.e., physical contact with ice-cold porcelain — is patently more injurious.

Men counter that this hazard is a function of women's approach to the seat, not of men's departure from it. Men argue that every approach to the seat should be regarded as a fresh approach, with nothing to be taken for granted except the routine necessity of visual inspection. Failure to look before sitting, men argue, violates the principle of caveat qui sedet, *"let the sitter beware."*

Women reject this principle. Women posit a principle of ground zero or middle C or home base — that is to say, a point of return that provides stability, a center: the seat down.

Men point out the wasted effort that men's adherence to this latter principle would entail. First, no matter who had used the facility last, men intending to engage in activity number one would have to raise the seat. Then, no matter who might be using the facility next, men having engaged in activity number one would have to lower the seat again. If five male usages occurred consecutively — that is, with no female usage intervening — then ten raisings or lowerings of the seat would be performed, not one of which was necessary. Furthermore, men point out, it is a greater burden on men to bend over and raise the seat, than for women to lower the seat on their way down — because women are shorter, and because lowering-while-sitting is a more natural, gravitational motion.

Women counter that if men want to talk about natural motions, they should go teach their grandfathers to eat eggs.

Men counter that women have that saying — namely, "Teach your grandmother to suck eggs" — all wrong, not only the terms of it but the point of it.

Women counter that who are men to tell them how a saying goes? Women assert that they have just used a women's saying; men may have in mind some men's saying.

Men counter that "Teach your grandmother to suck eggs" is not a men's saying, it is a folk saying that has been passed down by peoples of both genders for centuries, and that the trouble is that women never get sayings right.

Women counter that if women never get sayings right, then how can they have been involved in the passing down of this characterization of women as egg suckers that men have dragged into a discussion of the disposition of seats as an aspect of the natural order of things, which is seats should be down.

Men counter that how would women like it if men engaged in activity number one without raising the seat.

Women counter that the only reason seats ever have to be raised in the first place is that men cannot perform activity number one with sufficient accuracy.

With that, the argument ends. Because men — out of natural graciousness — refrain from voicing the final, clinching point.

To wit: Everyone knows that the only reason women complain about men's behavior during number-one activity — particularly with reference to ice-coldness — is that women will never get over the fact that women, unless they are extraordinarily nimble-footed, cannot write their names in the snow.

How to Get a Lot out of Opera

I GUESS everyone who keeps up with high culture knows about this already, but I was staggered a while back when I read in the *New York Daily News* that heckling was a big thing at the Metropolitan Opera. In fact one night when Renata Scotto made her entrance, reported the *Daily News*, "before she could open her mouth, a volley of boos, catcalls, and obscenities were hurled at her. . . . Of all the performing arts, opera seems first in encouraging baseball-stadium heckling."

I didn't even know the *Daily News* covered opera. And I thought the only connection between opera and sports was that the ideal person for the title role in *Otello* would be Franco Harris of the Steelers (who is half black and half Italian), if he could sing. Once I sat in the front row at the Met for a performance of *Die Meistersinger*. No boo-birds that night. What I was struck by was the elegance of my fellow front-row patrons' shushes.

You didn't hear them say anything low-rent like "Shaddap."

"*Ssht!*" they would go, piercingly. One bejeweled woman turned around and hissed to a heavyset man (who did look like a baseball fan, but not the rowdy type): "*Would you have the goodness not to rattle . . . and . . . wheeze!*"

"Would you have the goodness not to rattle . . . and . . . wheeze!" This — including ellipses — she hissed in one breath. A piece of work, that woman. I looked down the row at her and mouthed "*Bravissima*" (knowing, as I did, that "*Bravissimo*" is for a man) and winked, but she of course — quite visibly — made no response. To think that anyone in the same audience as that woman would hurl a catcall amazes me.

Now that a thousand dollars is so diminished a quantity (although anyone planning to make out a check to me for that amount should go ahead), opera is probably the only thing left, besides an occasional piano, that can get away with being "grand." And its devotees make those of baseball, liquor, and any combination of the two seem noncommittal. I knew a man who could not listen to Zinka Milanov without getting a nosebleed.

So how can opera have come to the verge of pop-bottle-throwing? I thought the least refined thing you could do at the opera was to lose concentration: to be among that certain number of operagoers who think the costumes and drapes are swell, and who recognize a given high or low note as really something, and who look forward sincerely to the "toreador song" (which occurs in all too few operas) or the appearance onstage of a live animal, but who are seldom able during the less rollicky stretches (all of *Die Meister-singer*, for example) to keep up with what is going on.

I myself, in fact, lost the thread of *Otello* one night years ago when the Met came to the Fox Theatre in Atlanta, where I then lived. The plot was well under way, and James McCracken as the Moor had already begun pitching and sobbing, when I realized I was trying to recapture in my mind's eye a certain piquant single I once saw Maury Wills hit.

Rather than risk musing thus irrelevantly (as I then thought) through a leap from a parapet, a death by tuberculosis, or a shout of *"Traditor!"* — no instant replay in opera, yet — I kept my mind on the show by resorting to two operagoing techniques that, though I felt they were not very elevated, are damn well more nearly grand than the raspberry.

The first of these is the less musical. It is a matter of taking fully into account the heft of an operatic exclamation and then imagining what a comedown it must be for these singers to have to go home after the last act and argue with loved ones (unless they have married with unusual bravura) or pass the time with agents, tradesfolk, and neighbors.

Surely a person who has just come in from crying *"Basta! Basta! Obbliggiornamento!"* to the heavens, with the full support of top-of-the-line hautbois, timpani, double bassoons, flageolets, and gongs, and while dressed in a golden robe and crown or a full suit of glistening feathers, finds it intolerable to have to go "Ah right, ah *right!"* or "So *you* say," or "Well I don't know, they'll probably nominate Mondale or somebody but . . ."

What does such a person do when at home? Quote from arias? Improvise in High German? Mutter *con agitazione?* Thrash about with a scepter?

These are, of course, bad aesthetic questions, and ought to be turned to only if you cannot keep your head in the opera, itself, by means of the second technique. The second

57

technique has the virtue that it focuses your attention on the action and the music; it just translates them into a recognizable life situation.

Otello, for instance, is waving his arms and hopping and demanding something of Iago, who seems to be putting him off.

OTELLO: What in the name of God am I doing out here on the stage of the Fox Theatre in this elaborate *bath*-rooobe?

IAGO: Oh! Don't worry, it's nothing nothing *noth*-ing.

OTELLO: And these unbelievable *shoe*-hoos!

IAGO: They're nice! They're nice!

OTELLO: The last thing I remember I was in this little bar and grill on *Cone* Streeeet.

IAGO: Um-hmmmmm, um-hm-hum-hm!

OTELLO: Eating an order of chicken . . . chicken . . . chick-ken . . .

IAGO: Cacciatore!

This procedure is not, it must be borne in mind, an end in itself. But if you stick with it you won't be woolgathering when the Walküre start going over the mountain with a "Yo-ho-to-ho-ho!" or something else on that order happens, something grand by any standard.

Nor will you be yelling "Choke! Choke!" or "Yabumya."

BLUE YODEL 8

HASKELL

One thing I emphasize when I speak to groups of men is that so-called performance anxiety is a myth. From time to time over the years, a man would tell a woman he had performance anxiety so that she would regard him as a challenge. Sometimes it worked. If it didn't, he told her he was just kidding and asked her if she would like another glass of wine.

A normal man can do anything. If he wants to. It's as simple as that. And normal men have traditionally taken this for granted.

Unfortunately women psychiatrists — on whom the performance-anxiety gambit has worked at some point in their lives — have started diagnosing "performance anxiety" in their men patients. And sometimes these patients believe them. That's why it is necessary that we as normal men get together — at the Century Club, for instance — and refresh ourselves as to basic principles. Such as, that a normal man can do anything he wants to do. And he always wants to. Unless he is tired.

When I speak to men's groups I usually illustrate my point by singing a blues song. Blind Sweet Papa Joe Tatum's "If Only All the Rest of Y'all Weren't Having Such a Fine Time Blues."

Now I went to Choate, Brown, and Harvard Law. My specialty was strikebreaking law until my firm started representing the Teamsters. I own beautiful vacation homes in four different military dictatorships. Furthermore I have this rather fluty voice and can't be bothered to keep time.

If I can get up before people and sing a blues song, then how can there be any such thing as performance anxiety? In normal men.

I define a normal man as one who can eat two hamburgers.

What to Do
on New Year's Eve–I

THERE comes a time in life when it is unseemly to awaken late in the afternoon of January 1 on someone's snooker table, naked save for a tiny conical hat (whose elastic strap has ridden up to just under your nose), shriveled tuxedo pants, and a crust of onion dip and confetti. In your productive middle years, you tend to feel not only your responsibilities but also your hangovers deeply: way down in the nucleoli of your every body cell, for up to three months. Furthermore you find those little hat-straps to be more and more irritating, even under the chin (even if you still have only one of those), and even *during* the party.

New Year's Eve becomes a time not to blow off steam, but to behave yourself. This realization may come as more of a relief than steam blowing does. "Nothing is more hopeless than a scheme of merriment," wrote Dr. Johnson. There is no American merrymaking, or merry faking, so forced and obligatory as a New Year's Eve party. There is also no hangover — not to dwell on this point — so profound as that induced by a lot of champagne on top of a lot of, say, bourbon and a number of sips of various fellow celebrants' apricot and artichoke and so on liqueurs.

What, then, is to be done on December 31? Should the day be ignored altogether? Or is there a way to ring out the old and in the new without leaving yourself with the feeling that you have spent forty-eight hours inside a gong? Let us consider some of the possibilities.

1. Ignore December 31 altogether. The trouble with this is that it may become a habit. If so widely ac-

knowledged a day as New Year's Eve can be ignored, then why not the following Monday? Why not every Monday? Why not February? Why not the entire new year? These are all good questions. If you hold a position of mature responsibility, it is better not to ask them.

2. Celebrate with a magnum of sparkling water, a bowl of light watercress dip, and some cauliflower sprigs. Unfortunately this pretty much comes under the heading of number 1.

3. Celebrate New Year's Eve, 1958. This seems worth a try, until you realize that it is not worth a try. You drank worse things in 1958 than you do now. And where are you going to find a pair of pink-and-black socks?

4. Dress up like the New Year and lie in a sensory-deprivation tank until midnight. The trouble with this is, what if it gets back to the people in the office? Or what if, being made to feel born-again, you never get back to the office?

5. Stay home, watch Times Square on television, and at midnight, instead of kissing thirty-four wives in one minute, kiss your own wife for thirty-four minutes. You need not feel maturely responsible for whatever happens next.

My New Year's resolution is to try number 5. It is too late to resolve to try it this New Year's Eve, however. This New Year's Eve, out of a mature sense of obligation, I am going to attend a party. Maybe a *bit* of champagne, but I intend to lay off the dip as soon as traces of it reach my first knuckles. And I will take the sensible precaution of placing a bit of adhesive tape under my nose.

BLUE YODEL 9

JESSE

I'll tell you what Miriam and I can't talk about. Warren Beatty. Warren Beatty almost destroyed our marriage one night.

Originally it was "Who do you find attractive in the movies?" Seems like an interesting question, right? Way for men and women to understand each other. Don't try it.

Miriam couldn't think of anybody. "I don't know any of them well enough," she said.

"No. Wait. Of course you don't!" I said. "That's not the point! But, like, for instance, somebody like Warren Beatty."

"Oh, no," she says. Wrinkles her nose.

"What?" I said to her. "You're not attracted to Warren Beatty?"

"No," she says.

"Yes you are," I say, "you just don't want to admit it."

"No I'm not!" she says. "And I don't know any women who are."

"What!" I say. "Warren Beatty has run through Natalie Wood, Joan Collins, Leslie Caron, Julie Christie, Diane Keaton, God knows who else, and he's not good enough for you or anybody you know?"

Now she's getting upset.

"Look," I say. "I'm not Warren Beatty. I don't know Warren Beatty. I don't imagine I have to worry about you ever meeting Warren Beatty. We're just, you know, talking about a guy on a screen. You can level with me."

She won't say anything.

"Okay!" I say. "Okay! Who are you attracted to? There's got to be somebody. I mean one big whole point of the movies . . . Don't get me wrong. I'm not saying you'd be a pushover for Warren Beatty. I'm not saying you're mooning over Warren Beatty. I'm not saying you admire Warren Beatty's life-style. I'm just saying, in your heart of hearts . . ."

She won't say anything.

"Okay. Never mind Warren Beatty, who . . . But never mind. There must be somebody."

"Well, okay," she says finally. "Ed Asner."

Ed Asner! She gets turned on by Ed Asner! She's twenty-eight years old and she claims she's hot for Ed Asner!

Hey. I like Ed Asner. Who doesn't like Ed Asner? But when Warren Beatty and Ed Asner run into each other somewhere, on or off the screen, I don't think it is Beatty who is thinking, "How does he do it?"

Ed Asner. Now every time I'm looking into Miriam's eyes I'm thinking . . .

Hey. I'm thirty-four years old! I've got hair! I work out! I'm married to a woman who is turned on by Ed Asner!

"Okay," I say to Miriam. "Ed Asner, to me, he looks like a good guy; no doubt about it. I'd love to have a few beers with Ed Asner. Probably rather have a few beers with Ed Asner than with Warren Beatty. But I'm not talking about that. I'm talking about, you know, somebody who — like, for me, I'd say, for example, Ann-Margret. You know. Does it for me."

"Whuh!" Miriam says. "Ann-Margret?" She looks at me like I said Peter Lorre.

"Of course Ann-Margret," I say. "That's the whole point of Ann-Margret. Why do you think they make Ann-Margret movies?"

And it's like I just destroyed the whole basis of our relationship. Miriam is appalled. Because I said Ann-Margret did it for me.

"Listen!" I say. "Come on. I'm not saying me and Ann-Margret would be compatible. I'm not saying there'd be any future in it. I'm not saying we'd have much to say to each other. I'm just . . . See, the whole point . . ."

Miriam wound up spending the night with her friend Wendy. Who I can't stand. Who now, whenever anybody brings the movies up, makes a point of saying how Warren Beatty thinks he's so cool.

I don't say anything.

I tell you what. People talk about a ménage à trois. How does anybody ever agree on the third party?

How to Sweat

ONE summer a man in Plains, Georgia, asked me what I did for a living. His was an outdoor job, tending worms for Jimmy Carter's cousin Hugh, the gentleman worm farmer. I said, "Write." He said, "I bet you can do that in the shade."

I can. And I know I ought to be grateful. But in the summer I like to get out every so often and sweat. Sure, it's possible to incur a little dampness while at the typewriter. According to Ben Jonson, "Who casts to write a living line, must sweat." But what I'm after actually comes down your back in living rivulets.

There are points to be raised against sweat. It stings sunburn, it streaks your glasses, and it gets in your eyes. But it feels better on your skin than any of those gunky suntan lotions whose revolutionary new ingredient is oil of kipini nut. Personally, I would want to spend some time on the isle of Uai, or wherever it is that the kipini nut grows, checking into all the properties of the kipini nut before I rubbed it on myself in large amounts. There are nuts over there on those islands that can turn a middle-class American into something that looks like a year-old carrot. Whereas with sweat, you know where it comes from.

Sweat is the essence of yourself, at least as much as speech is. And it's cleaner than speech. Good, honest sweat. You can get out in the garden and bend over to weed, and literal brow sweat will drip off onto the loam. The vegetables like it.

I remember one time, when pitchers got to hit in the American League, Vida Blue was perspiring so freely that when he slid into the dry dirt at third he came up muddy. That was *personal* mud.

Sweat is the body's way of saying to the sun, "Hey, you can't parch my man here. You maybe can fry him, but he won't dry-roast. He is going to have some gravy." When the sun is beating down and you're pumping sweat right back at it, you are *responding*, going one on one with the sun.

The word *sweat* suggests a heavy swipe across a wet brow, but it also calls to mind *swell*, *whet*, *suet*, and *sweet*. Hamlet maintained that no one would "grunt and sweat under a weary life" if he didn't fear the unknown hereafter. But that was years ago. These are modern times we're in now. Microcircuits or something — ingeniously carved by computerized laser beams from the now-synthesized shell of the kipini nut — do our grunting and toiling, unless we're stuck with a hands-on, worm-farm job. We sit around building up stale stuff in our pores. When we break a sweat, when all our little integumentary dams burst, we sweat out flus, hangovers, anxieties, curdled spite. We convert all those things into a form that rejoins nature.

In the summer, then, I suggest that you sit out in the sun somewhere, maybe on a boat, where the sun can get at you. Move around enough so that the sweat seeps down into your joints. Drink enough beer to make sure the sweat wells don't run dry. Feel yourself becoming organically lubed.

I also recommend that you get out and play tennis or dash about in some other manner until your shirt is sopping.

Then on the way home, stop by the cool convenience store for juice and Absorbine Jr. Your shirt will stick to your back and chill you better than any air conditioning. When you get home the sweat will be crusty on you, so take a shower. Sweat comes off pleasingly with soap and water.

When you finish showering, you may find yourself unable to get entirely dry because you're doing some après-shower sweating. Go with it. Beads of moisture look good on a person. If you're not alone, incidentally, here's a tip: Nothing goes better between two bare people than sweat. You won't know whose is whose.

BLUE YODEL 10

ROD

Marisa rejects being expected to "do for" men. So she does for plants.

We have eighty-four plants. Marisa talks to them, and they nod. . . .

We have the only apartment I know of that has to be raked.

How Men Tell Time

BLUE YODEL 11
ABBO AND VAN

ABBO: *You know that joke you told me? Why does it take longer for a woman . . . ?*

VAN: *Yeah.*

ABBO: *I'm telling it to Dean and Monte. Dean and Monte haven't heard it. I'm telling it to Dean and Monte: "You know why it takes longer for a woman to reach orgasm than a man?" Right?*

VAN: *Right.*

ABBO: *And Monte says, "No. Why?" Right?*

VAN: *Right.*

ABBO: *And I start, "Who the f . . ." The punch line, right?*

VAN: *Right.*

ABBO: *And Grace pops up. Grace. I don't know where from. Around the corner. All of a sudden, Grace. Right? And I think, rrrrrrk, "Grace does not want to hear this joke." I'm right in the middle — "Who the f . . ." — and here's Grace and I'm thinking, "Grace will not like this joke." Right?*

VAN: *Right.*

ABBO: *And — but I've gone too far with it. I can't think of some new second half of the punch line right on the spot that Grace won't hate. Right?*

VAN: *Right.*

ABBO: *I mean Grace is not a shrinking violet. Grace is, you know, you can hang out with Grace. Grace likes a joke. But I'm thinking, Grace may not — Grace won't like this joke. Right?*

VAN: *Right. Even Grace.*

ABBO: *Exactly! And it's a shame! Even* Grace *won't like this joke. And she* should. *Because, this joke — the thing is, a woman may not realize about this joke, that when a man tells this joke, he feels, like, the poignance of it. Right?*

VAN: *Absolutely.*

ABBO: *And I'm talking — I mean the double-*edge *poignance. I mean this joke goes two ways! At least! It does! This is not a, you know, a like a pig joke. I mean, on the surface it is. And — hey, I like a good pig joke. But this — it sounds like, to a woman, it — that's the problem.*

VAN: *Right there.*

ABBO: *And the bad thing is, you know, Grace — I can't, with Grace I can't just stop in the middle and say "Woops," you know, and she'll understand it is not for her ears. Right?*

VAN: *Right. Not with Grace.*

ABBO: *That's the thing. With Grace — she likes a joke. You can say — like, for instance, here's a joke I told to Grace. No, wait! Grace told this joke to me. The joke, you know, the black guy goes into the Cadillac dealer, right?*

VAN: *Yeah?*

ABBO: *You didn't hear this joke? Black guy goes into a Cadillac dealer, you know, walks in, and the guy in the showroom — very snotty, right, the guy looks at this black guy, and, you know, we're talking new Cadillacs, right? — and the guy says to the black guy, snotty, "Uhhm, are you thinking about buying a Cadillac?"*

VAN: *Yeah . . .*

ABBO: *And the black guy looks at the guy in the showroom, right . . . and says: "I'm gonna buy a Cadillac. I'm thinking about pussy."*

VAN: *Oh yeah, right, right.*

ABBO: *And anyway, Grace told me that joke. So Grace is not somebody who doesn't like a joke. With, like, pussy in it or anything. Right?*

VAN: *Yeah. Grace . . .*

ABBO: *Right. So, but anyway — this is . . . talk about poi-*

gnant. *This is a terrible moment. Because* I want Grace to hear this joke. But I'm afraid. *I'm afraid Grace will hate it! And I don't want to tell a joke Grace will hate! And — the terrible thing is, now, I'm right in the middle of the punch line,* "Who the f . . . ," *right? — and I . . . pause. 'Cause I saw Grace. Right?*

VAN: *Right.*

ABBO: *So now I'm dead. Grace heard me pause. She also heard the joke. So far.* So where is my way out?

VAN: *Yeah.*

ABBO: *You can't stop in the middle and start saying to Grace,* "Wait a minute, Grace — before I finish this punch line, you ought to know, this is a joke that I'm aware — I mean, this is a joke men tell each other and it, I mean, it does sort of strike at a certain male . . . knot or something, but — I mean men hear it and break up and it gives them a certain release . . . but men see the double-edge poignance of it." *Right? You can't say that in the middle of a joke. You can't say that* after *a joke. You can't say that* before *a joke. Right?*

VAN: *Right.*

ABBO: *Because, for one thing — just because men see the double-edge poignance of it, doesn't mean that they want to let on that they do. That'd defeat the whole . . . I mean you start* concentrating *on the double-edge poignance and you're right back into the knot. Hey! A woman ought to be able to hear this joke. And like it. In a way. But she won't. Even Grace. Right?*

VAN: *Even Grace.*

ABBO: *So, what I do — I can't stop and blush and run off. That'd be worse. I've got to push on through. I pause for a split second. And I look at Grace, who's expectant but is also sort of angling her head, you know, angling it and pulling it back slightly while looking at me out of one eye — you know,* "What is this I'm hearing?" *— and from Grace, I hate to see that look.*

71

VAN: *Because Grace . . . Yeah.*

ABBO: *But I push on through. I push on through with, you know, the punch line: "Who the fuck . . . cares?"*

VAN: *Right.*

ABBO: *And I wind up looking, with this sick smile, I wind up looking at Grace.*

VAN: *Yeah?*

ABBO: *And Grace didn't like it.*

What to Do on New Year's Eve—II

OKAY. You're sitting home alone on New Year's Eve with auld lang syne on your hands. What do you do?

1. Get out your Scottish dictionary and look up *auld lang syne*. You could dig around for hours without finding your Scottish dictionary. Get out your Scotch.

2. Wear a lampshade on your head. I have seen people do almost everything at a party: fall down, get naked, fight, start fires, climb out of windows, and put big wet slices of warm roast beef down each other's shirts. But I have never seen anybody put a lampshade on his or her head.

Try it, and you'll see why. A lampshade has prongs that don't fit the human head (might fit a cat's, but a cat would hate it), and there are dead moths in there. Stuck to the sides. But not stuck very securely. You could breathe one into your nose.

3. Call up friends. One problem with this is, they may be having a party that they didn't invite you to. I don't know why; they just didn't. Even if they live several hundred miles away, which would explain (maybe) why you weren't invited, they probably won't answer their phone themselves. Someone whose voice you don't recognize, and probably wouldn't recognize even if it weren't thickened by debauchery, will answer and say:

"HARPY NOYERS!"

"Hello," you'll say. "I'm a friend of Griff and Betty's —"

"HOOPY NOO-WAH!"

"Is Griff or Betty —"

"HOPPAH NAW REE!"

There will be a sound like people throwing roast beef in the background and you will hear the phone hit the floor. Eat your heart out.

4. Get yourself organized for the months ahead. There are twelve of them. I won't list them here. You could take out twelve slips of paper, write the name of a different month on each one, and set them out neatly, in chronological order (I mean the order in which the months come during the year, not the order in which you wrote them on the slips, though it is a good idea to write them on the slips in the same order in which they come during the year, because otherwise you could forget March), on a desk or tabletop. Or the floor will do. Especially if you have fallen down.

Now. Take more slips of paper, a lot of them, and write on each one something that you intend to get done:

- Take up organ.
- Oil reels.
- Obedience classes — Mitzi.
- Winterize gazebo.
- Get racquetball racquet. (In your wording, you want to be terse and businesslike. Isn't there something redundant about "racquetball racquet"? You wouldn't say

"football foot." "Tennis tennis-ball." And isn't that a pretty la-di-da spelling — "racquet"? As in "leather jacquet," or "yacquety-yacque.")

- Europe. (But you don't want to be so terse in your wording that, when the month to get this thing done rolls around, you won't remember what it was you were going to do. *Visit* Europe? Reassess Europe's role in the world community today? Or does that say "Elope"? Use good handwriting.)
- Look into umbrella coverage.
- Get things straight with the Seebohms.
- Learn cook Indian.
- Add inch to chest.

And so on. Now sort these slips of paper into twelve piles of things you are going to get done each month.

But are you going to get them done? Probably not. There is not much point in embarking upon the new year by trying to fool yourself. And failing.

5. Come up with this great idea for a screenplay about this guy who doesn't have anything to do on New Year's Eve or anybody to do it with, right? And he's all alone, see, so he's sitting there thinking [*voiceover*]: "Hey, this would be a great idea for a screenplay: a guy who's all alone on New Year's Eve trying to think of an idea for a screenplay, or trying to think of something to do, I mean, or somebody to do it with, so he ..."

6. Turn over a new leaf. This is something anybody could stand to do. I don't care if you are a prominent religious leader or the world's greatest living cellist. It wouldn't hurt you to turn over a new leaf. But you need to be in a dynamic mood to turn over a new leaf, unless it is a tiny leaf — like, "Okay! From this day forward I will never again clip my fingernails except over a receptacle of some kind!" And if you were in a dynamic mood you wouldn't be home alone on New Year's Eve.

74

Furthermore: I, for example, am forty-two years old and I have never turned over a new leaf. Not on purpose. It's like wearing a lampshade on your head. Trying to do such a classic thing makes you self-conscious. You wonder, "Is this for real?" When something is classic, you can never think of an example of how it's done.

Maybe in the Greek myths. But you may not be able to put your hand on any Greek myths. I don't think you want to start looking for them on New Year's Eve, after you've already been through the whole house looking for a Scottish dictionary.

What if you did find, say, *The Iliad*? The Trojan Wars don't provide much of a model for a person sitting home alone. Unless you are the type of guy who gets up and goes out and kidnaps someone named Helen. If you are, you ought to turn over a new leaf.

BLUE YODEL 12

GABRIEL

They say guys who do great with all kinds of women, what they do is look at a woman like she's the most important thing in the world in their eyes.

Well, I don't want to lie. I just want to go up to her and say, "You're lookin' good, come on home with me." You know.

But I can't do that. If I did and she did, then I'd be going home with somebody who'd go home with somebody who just came up to her and said, "You're lookin' good, come on home with me." You know.

But that's what I want to do.

The Roosters Don't Like It

AN HOUR of time for an hour of daylight. If that wouldn't sound fishy to an unnumbed person, I don't know what would. How about an acre of space for an acre of prime bottomland? A gallon of volume for a gallon of honey? Time to trade time for light, the bland newscasters tell us two Saturday nights a year, in April and October, and we do. Without protest. It is the contemporary thing. It makes me nostalgic for the activist sixties, when I was living in Georgia among people who would not take Daylight Saving lying down.

In Georgia in those days, the question of ordained time was thrashed out where God meant for bedrock matters to be thrashed out: in the legislature. Under the federal Uniform Time Act, a state could opt out of DST from one year to the next, and plenty of Georgians annually resisted traipsing to and fro through time just to keep in step with complete strangers.

Maybe time is *supposed* to be a raw deal. If you mess with it, maybe it gets worse. In fact, held the traditionalists, so-called (*so-called* was a key political term in Georgia at that time) Standard Time was drastic enough: since Georgia was in so-called Eastern Time but was close to the so-called Central Time line, it was actually, according to what county you were in, only 8:41 or 8:38 or even 8:29 when the Boston–New York–Washington axis was trying to shove 9:00 down honest people's throats.

Why pretend that a Winged Chariot with endless corridors of shifting sand is subject to administrative fiat? Because these are dynamic, future-oriented times, said the daylight salvationists.

In the parliamentary battle between these two world

views, one solon charged that under Daylight Saving "the sun sets too long after dark." You may not think time is a moral issue. But for every extra dollar that some Atlanta wheeler-dealer made by peddling a water-ski-rope-bobber or some damned thing in the glare of artificially prolonged afternoon, there was one more rural schoolchild who probably got lost trying to find his way to the school bus in the pitch dark of so-called morning and was never seen again. And the converse could be put, and was.

The debate, it seemed to me, should have been staged as an outdoor pageant. There was a very successful one in the North Carolina mountains that depicted how Andy Jackson cleared out the Indians, a noble people who never harnessed tourism's potential. Today, when an imposing percentage of Americans in every state own a water-ski-rope-bobber and yearn to get enough of an edge on the economy to buy a new model, the issue of Temporal Relativity vis-à-vis the Spiritual Absolute may seem moot. But no more so than the Indian issue. In the eighties, it seems appropriate to reflect that a person might enhance his capital position, and hearken back to days of eternal verities, and also hearken back to days of modern, future-oriented dynamism, by getting himself commissioned to create a pageant along these lines:

At the crest of the highest hill in Georgia are gathered a myriad of interests — drive-in-theater operators, stockbrokers, poultry, airline-reservation clerks, schoolchildren, TV folk, farmers, Jaycees, and cattle. They fall into two camps, God's Time and Up-to-date Time, from which are heard, contrapuntally, the following cries.

GT: It ain't decent to go to the drive-in before dark!
UT: Do you want "Eleven Alively News" at 10:00?
GT: You want noon at 1:37?
UT: The Leisure Industry feels . . .
GT: You ever gotten up at 2:30 to milk?

77

UT: What can you know of jet fatigue?

The two camps advance upon each other menacingly until . . .
The Sun rises over the hill.

SUN: What on earth?

DIRT FARMER: It ain't natural. I get up at dawn every day anyway and when I do it under Daylight Saving it makes my day twicet as long and the roosters don't like it.

STOCKBROKER: No, listen here. In the summer when it's 4:00 PM here, unless we have Daylight Saving Time, it's 5:00 PM in New York. So when I call Wall Street to broke a stock at 4:45 here, the man I want to broke it to has left the office. I call his home and his wife says, "Wait a minute, I'll see if I can get him, he's out playing Red Rover, Red Rover with the children." Of course he is in no mood to deal. And by the time I get home, I have only two hours of daylight left to play Red Rover, Red Rover with *my* children. Surely you can see that?

DIRT FARMER [*cannily*]: Red *whut,* Red *whut?*

STOCKBROKER: There is no *talking* to these people!

COW: Uhmm, I don't know. Uhmm'but it looks like the feddle gummunt running ever'thing. Uhmm'but it can't run cows. And somebody said you ever had to get up at 2:30 to mmmmm'ilk? Mwell I jus want to know did anybody ever have to get up at 2:30 to be mmmmm'ilked?

CITY BUSINESSMAN: I appeal directly to the Sun! I represent EHEU-Georgia, the state affiliate of Extra Hour Enthusiasts United. And I would like to remind the Sun that Daylight Saving affords every citizen of Georgia an extra hour to water-ski or swim or boat or fish or go crabbing or ever what form of recreation he so may choose — and all in the Sun! I also sell boats.

DIRT FARMER: Now, wait a minute. You ain't gittin' twixt we'uns and the Sun. We is the ones that labors from kin till cain't.

TV PERSONALITY [*raised God knows where*]: *What* till *what?*

DIRT FARMER: Yessir. From when we jist kin see the Sun till we jist cain't. Yessir. And we ain't sittin' still for no satchel-totin' boorycrat to tell us when we kin and when we cain't. How 'bout it, Sun?

There is a pause.

SUN: Friends, your Sun is deeply moved by these expressions, on both sides, of confidence and love. What your Sun would ask is that you live in peace and harmony, under the Sun. Regarding this great and crucial question you bring before me, I find myself in no position to comment further publicly at this time. Your Sun has this morning accepted from the National Science Foundation a federal research grant of . . .

DIRT FARMER: The Sun hath come under a cloud!

CITY BUSINESSMAN: Want to buy a boat?

It may be objected that this pageant is too "down." Something brighter and more timely may be desired. For are we not enlightened enough today to recognize that there are, in the true sense, no opposing camps? Surely daylight, time, business, farming, East, West — matter itself, for that matter — are all pretty much a matter of each other. Most of matter, we now know, *is* daylight, in the sense of space. As in the song

> *When was the last time you've seen us*
> *In the dark nibbling each other's ears?*
> *We've put lots of daylight between us*
> *Over the last few years.*

Daylight is like time in that something we would like to change about both of them is: they make us look older. What we might have in the pageant is a scene in which we turn forty, and the not necessarily reliable Time-Light

79

chorus intones, "Well . . . you . . . don't . . . *look* . . . forty."

Now through multimedia effects we flash forward thirty years, to the chorus filing past us and intoning, "Well . . . they . . . certainly . . . don't . . . *look* . . . dead."

But we deceased don't let it go at that. We come back with something. We have squirreled away enough daylight in our time that we are able to burst incandescent for just one instant and crack: "Okay, y'all, be cool. We got to roll around heaven."

And sink back down.

And then what?

Then we spring right spang back up, fling out our arms limberly, and dance! Risen like a water-ski-rope-bobber released from the deep, we sing of how dark, musty, exhaust-filled time will henceforth become moment upon moment lit so well from within that without is no real problem. Old time is restituted, new time saved, indeed, for we have pulled it off, we have come to light, we have outslicked Ramona in the Dark Glasses.

Here's what happened: We caught a glimpse of that certificate the chorus was handing around. It gave the time of our passing as 2:15 AM the last Sunday of April. *And there is no such time.*

BLUE YODEL 13

HARRY

Before she got a job she was always complaining: "Every time I want you to do something with me, Harry, you say you have to work."

I would say, in a level tone of voice: "That's just clearly not true. I could bring anybody in off the street, and they could listen to what you just said, and they would say, 'That's not really the case.' For one thing, I did something

*with you yesterday. For another thing, I'm not just saying I
have to work, I do have to work. Be reasonable."*

*And she would look at me and say: "I wish you could hear
yourself, Harry. 'Be reasonable'!"*

*You know, a woman can take something you just said and
repeat it back to you in this tone of voice like it's obviously
exactly the kind of statement Adolf Hitler always made.*

*" 'Be reasonable,' " she'd say. And she'd look like I
just — like anybody could plainly see that I just hit her with
an ax. And then she'd say, "I'm telling you how I feel,
Harry." And then she'd look at me like she just said something that any decent human being would realize was the
bottom line of the universe.*

*And I'd say — I tell you what I wouldn't say. I wouldn't
say, "So?" For some reason, it is universally regarded as fas-
cist to say "So?" to a woman who has just told you how she
feels. I accept that. But, say, maybe I would say something
like, "Okay. But . . ."*

*And she would explode. "But that doesn't mean anything
to you, Harry!" she'd say. "Because men don't know anything about sharing feelings!"*

*So then she got a job and now every time I want her to do
something with me, she has to work. So I complain.*

*And she says: "Now you know how it feels, Harry! So just
don't complain!"*

*So I say: "Wait a minute. You always complained. Now
you know how it . . ."*

*She says: "You're critical! You're not supportive! You
don't want me to work! It's all right for you to work. But
when I work, Harry, you feel threatened!"*

*So I say: "Wait a minute. You say men don't know any-
thing about sharing feelings. But when I try to get you to
feel the way I felt when you felt the way you used to feel, let
alone try to tell you how it feels for me to feel the way you
used to feel, you want me to shut up and feel the way I used
to feel when you complained all the time and the way you*

used to feel when you complained all the time — and yet you won't let me complain!"

Only I don't say that. Because I get lost about halfway through.

It's no contest. Women can bitch better than men. Women can hold down a job and still bitch better than men.

Secrets of Rooting

Have you been wondering when something is going to come along the way rock 'n' roll came along? I think it has, and I'm afraid I'm going to have problems with it. Before I reveal what it is, I feel I should explain about the problems.

The most unforgettable date I ever had — in fact, the only date I ever had for which I will never forgive myself — was the only date I ever had with a cheerleader.

It wasn't her fault. Not at all. In fact . . . but no. That is the one tangle of recollections that will never be coaxed out of me. Twelve of the world's finest cheerleaders could be crying

> *Come on, tell us!*
> *You're our man!*
> *We'll understand it*
> *If anybody can!*

and I wouldn't let out a peep.

The incredible thing that I did, the even more incredible reasons why I did it, the dreams afterward . . . And I had been around a little bit by then. I had already gone steady with a cocaptain of majorettes. But a cheerleader, somehow . . .

Don't get me wrong. I didn't do anything that makes me in retrospect want to kick myself for being so chauvinistic. On the contrary. But you don't want to know. You wouldn't be moved to cheer, I can tell you that.

Ever since that date, I have realized that I suffer from some kind of complex with regard to cheering. The root problem may be that I was reared (too heady a word) to believe that pride goeth before — segues into — a fall. At any rate, the very idea of cheering makes me blush.

I remember one time I was in a pro-football locker room when one player said to another, "Lend me two bits."

"Hey," said the second player, "I'm from the country. What's two bits?"

"A quarter," said a third player, whom we will call Dave.

"How do *you* know?" asked the second player. "You're from the country too."

> *"Two bits, four bits,*
> *Six bits, a dollar.*
> *All for Dave,*
> *Stand up and holler.*

I learnt it from the poem," Dave replied.

I could never have said such a thing. If my name were Dave and I were to break into a cheer for myself, it would probably go something like this:

> *Gimme a* D!
> *D!*
> *Gimme an* A!
> *A!*
> *Gimme a* V!
> *V!*
> *Gimme an* E!
> *E!*
> *Whatcha got?*
> *Exactly!*

But I am getting ahead of myself. (Which is not to say that I feel I should be behind myself. At least not solidly.) What I set out to do was find out how cheers around the country reflect the regions whence they spring. NATION'S DIVERSITY SEEN IN YELLS — that sort of thing. The Ethical Culture School in hard-boiled Manhattan, for instance, had a cheer that went

> *Strong as a lion,*
> *Swift as a vulture.*
> *Rah rah rah,*
> *Ethical Culture.*

And Louisiana State University has a Cajun food cheer:

> *Hot boudin,*
> *Cold coush-coush*
> *Come on, Tigers,*
> *Poosh poosh poosh.*

(Boudin is a sausage made out of blood and rice and one thing or another. Coush-coush is a mush made of fried cornmeal batter.)

A synagogue outside Washington, D.C., had as its pep raiser

> *Aleph, beth, gimel, daleth,*
> *Temple Sinai's really solid!*

Presumably I would send out feelers across the length and breadth of the land and learn that Alaskans holler

> *Seal whiskers, whale blubber, oh oh oh,*
> *Hit 'em like an ice floe, Esquimaux!*

and that Iowans shout

> *Iowans can,*
> *Iowans will.*
> *This is a pretty boring cheer probably, but*
> *Kill Kill Kill.*

84

When I poised to plunge into my researches, however, I ran into a kind of block. I didn't know anybody in Alaska or Iowa. "Don't give me that," I tried to tell myself. "Hey! You've researched all kinds of things, with enormous pep!" Still there was this block. There was the visage (just for starters) of Ramona. That cheerleader. Her name wasn't Ramona, but she looked like she would have a name like that: dark, glowing. Oh, Jesus.

I called the International Cheerleading Foundation. The International Cheerleading Foundation, I thought, will offer help. In fact, I thought, as soon as I say (not wanting to use my own name in case Ramona might be working there) "This is Dave," the person answering the International Cheerleading Foundation's phone will lift my spirits with a yell:

> *All right, Dave!*
> *The ICF*
> *Gonna save save save*
> *You from yourse'f.*

But I was wrong. The ICF could tell by the tone in my voice that I was no Dave, I was the guy Ramona filed the report on. What the ICF did was promise to send me a bunch of cheers, and then not do it. And when after three weeks I called again, the ICF sent me a *few* cheers. Which depressed me. One of them (identified as a "general chant") looked exactly like this:

> *BETTER EAT YOUR*
> *WHEATIES AND*
> *DRINK YOUR JUICE*
> *'CAUSE THE EAGLES ARE IN TOWN*
> *AND THEIR CUTTIN' LOOSE,*
> *BETTER TAKE THEM VITAMINS*
> *AND PUMP THEM WEIGHTS,*
> *'CAUSE YOU POOR TURKEY'S LOOK*
> *JUST LIKE-EAGLE BAIT!*

Set aside my apparently being included among the "turkey's." How could I be lifted by an outfit that spells and punctuates and scans like that? Spelling, punctuation, and scansion are *important* to me. They weren't, I recall, to Ramona.

After concluding that the ICF was not for me, I learned that it is not the only cheerleading organization. Two former cheerleaders (I relate to them very well on a *friendly* basis) told me that there are two competing groups known as the American Cheerleaders Association and the National Cheerleaders Association. The latter promotes precision execution and stark classical gestures; the former is the one to be affiliated with if you want to flirt from the sidelines and "be prissy and goosey."

My knees, when I heard that, grew weak. Prissy and goosey is exactly what Ramona was. (Her two best friends were *named* Prissy and Goosey. I know she must have told them about that night. I know how they must have reacted.) *And* dark and glowing. I didn't try to find either the ACA or the NCA. I listened gloomily as Slick Lawson of Nashville recalled how the cheerleaders of his high school would come back from cheerleading camp every year with several new, highly complex cheers, which they would swing into proudly. And the crowd would sit in silence. The new cheers were too complicated. The cheerleaders would sigh, and go back to

> *Strawberry ice cream,*
> *Huckleberry pie,*
> *V-I-C-T-O-R-Y.*

Ordinarily I would have taken a bit of Americana like that and gone extrapolating off into a wide-ranging political thesis, which would explain Ronald Reagan and any number of other phenoramona. I mean pheromone . . . I mean Ramona.

Pheromones. You know what pheromones are? (Look

them up. I'm too run-down to explain. I already explained boudin.) Ramona had them. Pheromones. Every time Franklin Roosevelt comes into a conversation I think (with what kind of self-laceration you may or may not be able to imagine), "We have nothing to fear but pheromones themselves."

I bet that on about the fifth date she would have gone through some of her cheers for me with her whole uniform on (saddle oxfords! saddle oxfords!) except the pants! Or the sixth date anyway. Seventh. What does it matter now?

I am sorry. I realize I am being sexist and objectionable. There are male cheerleaders. Cheerleaders of any sex are not things to be ogled and drooled over, any more than . . . congresspersons are.

But I can't help it. When I was in high school, cheerleading was the only erotic thing that girls were officially encouraged to do. And, by heaven, they did it. Especially Ramona.

My children will not grow up with anything like the morass of feelings that I have about cheerleaders. At my children's school there are no cheerleaders. Can you imagine that? All the students, male and female, *play* sports. They have to. To my children, a cheerleader is a dated thing.

Dated! Ah!

I'll never get over Ramona. Ramona, and certain other moments. You know how there are looks you remember all your life? Often these are looks that you exchanged with people you didn't even know very well. In my case two of those looks — set aside anything that may or may not have passed between Ramona and me — involved cheering.

There was the time when I was a senior in high school. I was on the sidelines, for some reason, during a game my school won, a regional play-off. I myself was not on the team. We don't have time to go into that here. But I was down there on the sidelines for some reason with several other nonplaying students, and when our quarterback ran for a big touchdown, I *flung* myself into the air. A spontaneous cheerleader's move. I may never have jumped that high before in my life, and I certainly haven't since.

At my apex, I caught another student, a younger one, staring at me in disbelief. There I was in my abandon, and I realized, in midair, that my abandon was not cool. I should have been making stark classical gestures, I suppose. My abandon has not been the same since.

Skip ahead to my senior year in college. That year I was elected Alternate Mr. Commodore. Just out of the blue. I didn't run for it, not with my complex. But our team, Vanderbilt University, was the Commodores, and what Mr. Commodore did was wear what passed for a commodore's uniform, including one of those hats like half a bellows with feathers, and wave a sword and join in the rooting on the sidelines. The alternate filled in when Mr. Commodore was sick.

My year, he was sick once. For a basketball game. I filled in. Do you know what that entailed? It entailed, for one thing, holding a cheerleader by the thighs. She put her feet on my thighs and I grasped hers, after doing I don't know what with the sword, and she stood out from me at a forty-five-degree angle.

And I got into it. For over an hour I forgot Ramona. I went so far as to do something that no Mr. Commodore, to the best of my knowledge, had done before. With the score tied and the Commodores bringing the ball downcourt, I yelled bloodcurdlingly (I say it who shouldn't) and galloped the length of the court alongside the Commodores with the sword pointed straight ahead. And they scored. And the fans went wild.

And I came running back and the cheerleaders embraced me, sword and all. And here is the look I still remember: One particular cheerleader, fresh and sweaty, looking me full in the eyes with . . . joy. Complicity. A full welcome into the world of spirit and pep.

And do you know what I did? I blinked. I geared down. I knew in that moment that the kid who had given me that entirely different look back in high school was right. I knew that, in fact, my date with Ramona had been destiny telling me something. I knew that if I took one more step into the world of pep and spirit and that *kind* of thigh holding, I would never attain intellectual distinction. I would never write for the better magazines. I would never author a book.

And now let me tell you the one significant thing that my crabbed researches have uncovered. The new thing that is coming, the thing that I predict will sweep the country the way pelvismania did in the fifties, is this: Self-cheering.

Not a good term for it. Autorooting? Better terms will be coined. But my informant in Chapel Hill, North Carolina — Page Seay, who is twelve — reports that the kids in his school are into a kind of self-boosting rap cheer. Here are two examples.

A, O,
What's the matter with your Afro?
It don't grow.
It need some Vigoro.
Look at mine.
It's so fine.
Look how it shine, shine, shine.

Kool-Aid, Kool-Aid,
Hey, Kool-Aid, Kool-Aid, um.
You think you're hot.
Honey chile, I know I'm hot.
Um. You think you're cool.
Honey chile, I was born cool.
Um. You think you're fine.
Honey chile, I know I'm fine.
Just take a look at this behind.

These cheers started with black kids, but all the kids (girls and boys) are doing them now. I suppose the phenomenon derives from Muhammad Ali; dancing in the end zone; TV commercials; the self-absorption of the computer and video-game generation. I believe it will sweep the country.

After all, isn't Ronald Reagan's basic platform "Hey, I'm a big, good-looking guy. I need a lot of sleep. I shot down a Libyan plane. *In* my sleep"? Jimmy Carter was always worrying. Striding. Agonizing. Ronald Reagan is simply proud. Winking. Someday he is going to pop up on television saying:

> *"Ron's my name.*
> *I communicate.*
> *If you don't get it,*
> *Then you don't rate.*
> *High side, supply side,*
> *Only side is my side.*
> *You*
> *Shut*
> *Up!"*

And when you go to visit your mother, she will fling open the door, jut her hip, and exclaim:

> *"My kids don't call me, but I don't care,*
> *'Cause I look so foxy in my silver hair.*
> *See me coming, say, 'Uh-oh, who —*
> *Whose old lady, sweet momma, are you?' "*

As I say, I will have trouble swinging with this. But it is coming. It's perfect for schools where watching others cheer for others is . . . dated.

And I am afraid that some people are going to be swept away by self-cheering. The way previous generations have been swept away by hooch, by rock, by drugs. Cheering can be a consuming thing. I met a man not long ago whose mother in her youth was a cheerleader in upstate New York. His mother, he said with a sigh, used to do the locomotive.

You take a locomotive and you take it slow:
P [slow chugging motion],
O [slow chugging motion],
U [slow chugging motion],
G [slow chugging motion],
H [slow chugging motion],
K [slow chugging motion],
E . . .

The misfits of the next ten years or so are going to be those who have had an experience such as I had with Ramona. The blessed will be those with short names.

BLUE YODEL 14

J.J.

I was having trouble making a commitment. I came back from visiting Lisa and went to bed with Mary. And I couldn't get it up. And I thought: "I'm so much in love with Lisa I can't get it up with Mary!" And that made me feel so good I got it up.

Why Wayne Newton's Is Bigger Than Yours

SOME people have big ones; some people have little ones. Women have been shorted on them. Nobody really wants to know — but, on the other hand, everyone *does* want to know — how his stacks up next to the other fellow's. It's not so much the size of them as what you do with them and what goes along with them. (Sure!) There is a taboo against revealing them.

Salaries.

Not sexual organs. That's a different matter. For instance: If inflation in, say, sports had hit sexual organs the way it has hit salaries, there would be utterly no rationale for preventing women reporters from conducting interviews inside men's locker rooms. Because every time you opened the door to a men's locker room, sexual organs would bob out into the hall.

Here is the deal: I have been offered a sum of money (none of your business how much; anyway, less than Burt Reynolds makes per *hour* — but I am taller than Burt Reynolds) to reflect upon some figures put together by David Harrop, author of *World Paychecks: Who Makes What, Where and Why*. And I am going to, though it opens up a can of worms.

In his book, Harrop tells us, for instance, that a New York City sanitation worker makes three times as much as the chief of staff of the Indian army (and yet the chief keeps his office picked up); that the president of Sri Lanka makes $243 a year (plus perks); that a consultant to a multinational corporation can make $2,000 a day; that Paul McCartney earned, or anyway took in, $48,200,000 in 1980. (One record-company exec to another: "There's good news and bad news. The good news is, Elvis is dead and his albums are selling like hotcakes. The bad news is, Glenn Miller has just reappeared and wants all his royalties.")

What Harrop has done is to divide various people's annual incomes by 2,080 (52 weeks times 40 hours) to ascertain their hourly wage. Since the average drug pusher (estimated $72.11 an hour), for instance, probably does not punch a time clock, that methodology can be quibbled with, but it does point up some startling contrasts. I think we can get down to the nub of this whole discussion by noting that, according to Harrop's figures, Wayne Newton makes $5,769.23 an hour and the average general-duty nurse, $5.93.

Wayne Newton is the economic (if not the musical) equivalent of 972.89 nurses! What does that say about American values? How can we justify a Vegas warbler's making almost 100,000 percent more per hour than a Florence Nightingale?

One way of looking at it, of course, is this: If it were the other way around, you might wake up in a hospital, feeling bad enough already, and there, leaning over your bed, would be Wayne Newton, all in white.

But a great deal remains to be said. I have been reading Freud, Marx, Norman O. Brown, both Adam Smiths, George Gilder, John Kenneth Galbraith, Ayn Rand, and Kropotkin industriously, and watching Lee Iacocca on television whenever I take a break, and I have come up with no easy answers. I do have one concrete proposal: that the average IRS agent's income ($10.81 per hour, according to Harrop) be changed to a certain fixed percentage of mine after taxes. Eighty percent, say. Thus, if I make $40,129 and am allowed enough deductions to keep $40,000 of that, the agent gets $32,000 (low enough so he doesn't lose his edge against the fat cats but high enough that he can take me out to lunch). The objection might be made that since $32,000 a year works out to $15.38 an hour, my proposal would increase the cost of government. Let it be amended, then, to apply *only to that agent each year who gets to handle my return*. In which case, what the heck, make it 90 percent.

I have other, more complex, thoughts to share — or, actually (this economic thinking takes hold after a while), to sell.

When sports attorney Bob Woolf was trying — successfully, as it turned out — to win basketball star Larry Bird as a client, he made a pitch to Bird, who was then still a student at Indiana State, and a group of Terre Haute men whom Bird had asked to advise him. "I was telling them about how much certain athletes were making, just to give them an idea of what we might expect for Bird's contract," Woolf later told the *New York Times*. "Then I mentioned Tommy John, the Yankee pitcher. Well, John is from Terre Haute. And these men said, 'Yeah, what does Tommy John make?'

"Then Larry ... interrupted. He said, 'Excuse me, Mr. Woolf, but Tommy John is a friend of mine. And I'd rather not know what he makes.'"

Probably, Bird's remark caused the Terre Hauteans in the room to mutter, "Darn!" But those men would have been loath to tell one another their own salaries, and if John had been present, no one would have been so rude as to ask him his. Most people don't know what their closest friends' salaries are. When I tell anyone my stipend for a given piece of work, even, I feel like a flasher. Why is that?

"Money is what all business is about," writes Michael Korda in his book *Power!*,

> and therefore it retains all the power of the central mystery of a religious cult. . . . In no single area of adult life do the rules of childhood apply so strictly as in raises. . . . If you ask how much someone else is getting, you will be told, "That doesn't apply," or "It's not your business," just as something other children were permitted to do was never a sufficient reason for being allowed to do the same thing ourselves. You will also be told to "be reasonable," "be patient" and to "try to understand our problems," advice liberally given to children by parents, teachers and headmasters and designed to make them feel guilty for even asking.

What if co-workers Jones and Smith go behind the boss's back and say, "I'll tell you mine if you'll tell me yours" — and find that Jones's is substantially greater than Smith's? It is a queasy, intimate moment. Jones feels like a teacher's pet, no longer able to gripe about the system along with the other kids, and Smith feels cheaply gotten. Of course, if Jones and Smith look at the big picture and consider what an agricultural worker in Cameroun makes ($40 a year), they both ought to feel like pigs. (It is not known whether or not any agricultural worker in Cameroun knows what Wayne Newton makes.)

There are deeper than strictly economic reasons why the average person draws a veil over his or her emolument. Freud associated money with excrement, the first medium of exchange. "Feces are the infant's first gift, a part of his own body which he will give up only on persuasion by someone he loves." (And then he grows up, becomes salaried, and money is what he gets for kowtowing to Mr. Dithers.)

See, I told you this isn't about sexual organs. That is to say, not about sexual organs alone. In *Life against Death*, Norman O. Brown argues that money represents, to the human psyche, not only BM but also death, guilt, magic, the child, Satan, the sacred, separation anxiety, "the aggressive fantasy of becoming father of oneself," and, too, the (detached) penis. Is it any wonder that we don't wave our incomes around lightly?

Even if you think of money as just paper, beads, smackers, mazula, simoleons, or something to bathe in, the way Scrooge McDuck does, the whole science of economics is strange enough. But if you regard your paycheck as an excremental dead magical baby-devil holy estranged pushy autopaternal pecker, then you wonder whether the bottom line (as they say) of economics was not drawn best by David Stockman: "None of us really understands what's going on with all these numbers."

In fact, at one point in my researches, I decided: Fuck it, I'm a Marxist.

A Marxist even though I would personally rather be alienated, as Marx said capitalist workers are, than herd sheep, which is more or less — as I understand it — what precapitalist workers did. That is just the way I am.

And a Marxist even though I discovered, in *Marx for Beginners*, that "Marx remained in London for the rest of his life, in the direst poverty (three of his children died through lack of medicines), continuing to write revolutionary books and articles."

"Wait a minute," I thought when I read that. Why couldn't a man with Marx's education and moneyed background *dabble* in capitalism or burglary or sell his whiskers or write a thriller under a pseudonym or *something* to keep his kids alive? However, I didn't want to make the kind of judgment my father did in refusing to read the poetry of Edgar Allan Poe on the grounds that Poe had married a teenager and devoted himself to debauchery while allowing her to die of consumption. That was unfair to Poe, I later learned; and, at any rate, my father didn't read the poetry of anybody else, either.

Marx*ism* applies far more directly to the matter of children dying in poverty than capitalism ever did, at least until Marx came along. And Marx made clear one reason nice people don't vaunt their salaries: Salaries are not only inequitable, they're unnatural.

Capitalism, Marx said, is obsessed with money as a thing in itself, though in itself money is useless and won't get you into heaven, which Marx didn't believe in, anyway. (Marxists pride themselves on their materialism and call capitalism idealistic because it supposes that man's just reward cometh not on this earth. Capitalists argue that their system has provided the greatest material rewards and that Marxism's vision of universal earthly parity is too idealistic. My own idea of heaven is one of ideal materialism: being married to a nurse who makes $5,769.23 an hour.)

Instead of working directly for their own needs, Marx said, people under capitalism sell their labor for money to exploitive types who invest the vigorish in pork futures.

(Little Richard is somewhat different. Little Richard works for money but also for Jesus; and recently, I am told, he stopped in the middle of a recording session and turned his back on the Christian businessmen who were standing by, prepared to move his product. Dismayed, the businessmen approached him warily. "Little Richard shall not sing another note!" he cried. "Until he gets some *bobby-cue!*" Marx didn't anticipate Little Richard.)

So people become alienated from their work (as well as their pork); it's just something they do for a buck — or, if they are James Watt when he was secretary of the interior, for $33.47 an hour and the chance to dispossess little bunnies and bluebirds. Marx felt that people should be able to work for their own enjoyment.

"*Yeah,*" I thought. Why should I have to write all this stuff about money and then sit home, waiting for the check, and then take it to the bank and stand in line and get some cash, and so on, in order to be able to buy some barbecue? When I could *eat barbecue for a living.*

Be at a party, and somebody says, "What business you in?"

"I'm in barbecue eating."

"That right?"

"Yep. What's your field?"

"I'm in baby-animal petting. Just got back from the Coast, took the red-eye in. I was petting weimaraner pups out there."

But then I realized it couldn't be that simple. To make a living eating barbecue, I'd probably have to raise pigs. Which, although it would require less legwork than raising sheep, I wouldn't enjoy. (There is another question of exploitation here, with regard to the fact that barbecue demands a lot of a pig. On the other hand, if it weren't for barbecue, there would be a lot less demand *for* pigs.) And I doubt I could raise pigs and also find the time to make halfway decent beer, so I'd have to trade a pig to somebody else

97

who was good at beer, and what is a six-pack worth in pork? You're comparing apples and oranges there. Before you know it, you're reduced to printing up little certificates, each one of them worth a pig, and minting little coins, each one worth a chitlin or a quarter, and soon you have to have bankers and economists and *The Kiplinger Tax Letter*.

Of course, Kropotkin said no, the way to go about things would be for people to produce what they enjoyed producing, and it would all go into a common storehouse from which all people would take what they enjoyed using. I believe, in fact, that the Hutterites do organize things that way. My hat is off to them.

But if everybody in the world were a Hutterite, that would be a big storehouse. You'd show up with a herd of pigs and stand in line behind a lot of other pigs and pigherds, and sheep and shepherds, and litters of kittens and guys trying to pass themselves off as catherds. . . .

"There's no such thing as a catherd."

"Yeah? Who says?"

"Why don't you just get your cat spayed, man?"

"Because she and I happen to *enjoy producing* kittens."

. . . and radishes and radishers, and hats and milliners, and burly designated hitters bearing bundles of runs batted in, and bales of ziti schlepped in by somebody who just got a new pasta machine — and your pigs are trying to get at the ziti and the radishes and the hats and even, for some reason, the sheep — and when you finally get to the head of the line, the people on storehouse duty (who would rather be out producing movies) are saying: "Pigs! More pigs! Where we going to put all these *pigs*?"

"I don't know. I just want some beer, right away, please."

"All right. . . . Hey! Where you going?"

"Back to the beer department."

"No you don't. You'll get everything out of order. We already got twenty thousand fishing worms and a flock of geese loose back there. Hey, Vernon! Bring this guy out some beer."

And Vernon would be back there yelling, "I only got two hands!" but he'd be getting around to it, and then you'd remember:

"Oh, and one of those little deals for connecting a washing-machine hose."

"What do you mean, 'little deals'?"

"You know, those little round strips of metal with the holes in them and a screw that you tighten . . ."

"Aw, no. That's over in hardware. Hardware is in the Philippines."

"The Philippines! How'm I going to get to the Philippines?"

"Go on over to the Eighteenth Street annex and pick up a plane ticket. Take all you'd enjoy using."

"How'm I going to get to the airport?"

"Go over to the Third Avenue entrance and requisition a cab. Couple of 'em, if you like."

"I don't want any cabs! And I don't want any plane tickets! I want one of those little washing-machine-hose deals. I got to get back home and eat barbecue."

Of course, everybody in the world isn't a Hutterite. Everybody in the world is all kinds of things. There are people who enjoy producing *terrible* poetry, and there are people who enjoy using radio aerials to hit people with.

Call me a pessimist, but I don't care how well that warehouse was run, there would be terrorists kidnapping people from it and guys in white sheets burning crosses in front of it. And pretty soon the storehouse would be out of beer when you wanted it, so you'd be issued little chits to make sure you could get some beer when it came in, and then, after a while, you'd be saying, "Hey, give me some *more* chits."

"What do you want more chits for?"

"What do you mean, what do I want more for? 'Cause I'd *enjoy using* 'em."

"Well, we're out of chits."

"Out of chits! How can you be out of chits? I only got . . . How many chits does Vernon get?"

"That doesn't apply. And it's none of your business."

Maybe it is just my upbringing, but I keep going back to the Fall of Man. There Adam and Eve were, in the primordial free storehouse, the Garden of Eden. Just don't eat the apple of knowledge, right? Is that too much to ask? In Russia, you don't get to read *Playboy* or the Bible; in Eden, you don't get to eat the apple.

Here comes the snake (representing the root of evil, Satan, death, guilt, bad shit, and — hey, why not? — the detached penis), boogity, boogity. Make a long story short, Eve and Adam bite the apple. And start comparing figures. And feel *wrong*, somehow, and put on fig leaves. Which lead to pants.

This is crucial. Because one of the simple enjoyments of being an infant is carelessly taking a dump. But outside Eden, babies wear pants.

And the parent has to change the pants. This is not work that the parent does for enjoyment. The parent does not go into these pants the way the parent would go into the Kropotkinite storehouse. And yet the parent — who doesn't want the baby to get irregular and start hollering — *counts on* something being there. Unpins the diaper and says, "Uh-huh. I *thought* this was what I'd find. *Whew!*"

The infant notes an ambivalence. Something primo about this stuff — the parent carries it off somewhere, must save it for special occasions — but something unsavory about it, too. "Hm," the infant starts thinking, "I can turn out this shit forever. But what exactly is the deal here?"

Then the parents start teaching the baby to save it. He's been enjoying it, using it to bring loved ones to his bedside, playing mud pie with it when he's bored. Now they want him to hold it in until he can deposit it into a shiny, impersonal facility very like a bank. Everybody is proud of him when he does this, and then — *floosh!* — the stuff is gone. And the part of him that produced it gets covered back up, along with other things, by his pants (which in due time will have, in the rear, a wallet pocket).

So. It is little wonder that we don't wear our salaries on our sleeves. It is little wonder that people develop an aversion to the New York Yankees when their owner keeps saying, in effect: "Hey, I give these guys a whole lot of money. So I expect them to take a whole lot of shit and produce." And yet it is little wonder that people tend to rate themselves and other people by how much money they themselves make and by how much the others must make; the way they spend it, you'd think it was water.

Money is, in fact, a mess, and the more inflated and recessed it gets, the more the media are full of it and the more absurd the quantities become (the government now is talking trillions) and the more compelled people feel to think in terms of it.

Furthermore, this feces/devil/death/child/penis material is distributed around the world in such a way that millions of people starve, and yet a number of people now, even outside (*well* outside) rock 'n' roll, make more than $1,000,000 a year. One of the prices you have to pay for being a corporate bigwig is that the SEC requires that the bacon you bring home be made public. The whole world knows, therefore, that J. Peter Grace, chief executive of W. R. Grace and Company, made $1,486,000 one recent year — and $1,000,000 of that was a "special bonus," presumably designed to make him feel better about the fact that David Tendler, cochairman of Phibro Corp., was compensated to the tune of $2,669,000. Hey, I'm not saying I would get indignant if a board of which I was cochairman were to call me in and say, "How does $2,669,000 sound?" Probably, I would just say, "Well . . . And this year, can I take the company slogan off the side of my Rolls?" But if I were a Corp.,

I'd be embarrassed to *have* to compensate somebody that much for working for me.

"A man's got to live," John Belushi said, tongue in cheek, when told of the millions that were pouring into his pocket from movie work, which he was afraid was crap, organized around moguls' focus on the moola. Trying to stay tongue-in-cheek, he blew as much of it as humanly possible on shit that Edenized, bloated, and killed him.

The first time I ever thought much about salary was when I happened to find out, sometime during puberty, that my father was making the same ($30,000) as Yogi Berra. That astonished me. I had always figured my father could make anything he wanted to (he made me a Bunsen burner once), but I had never seen him and Yogi Berra in the same light. I wondered whether I would ever have an income of that size. (Now, of course, $30,000 is less than the minimum major-league-baseball salary and is about what it would take to keep my family of four out of the poorhouse if under Reagan there were a poorhouse.)

My father was a wholesome capitalist. His first love was home building; his father was a carpenter-contractor with authoritative busted fingers and a knack for eyeballing square footage. But my father came of age in the Depression, so his father steered him clear of construction. Eventually, my father got into the savings-and-loan business: taking care of people's savings and lending them to other people to build houses with. He didn't love money (didn't even enjoy spending it) the way he loved wood, but he loved building his institution. There is no taboo against comparing annual statements. He wasn't getting a cut or anything, but he was always after more assets for his institution.

"We're getting our share," one of his colleagues told him.

"We want part of somebody *else's* share," he replied, and he said they were going to get it. My mother — though lei-

sure to her meant putting her feet up for one minute —
said my father was going to strive himself to death. They
both turned out to be right.

My father, however, would have printed a picture of Joe
Stalin on every one of his savers' passbooks if for some reason there had been no other way to get medicine for his
dying children. Of course, we would have heard about it for
the rest of our lives, via my mother: "There sits your father,
who had to become the only Bolshevik in the entire South-
east so you could have Aureomycin, and you can't behave in
Sunday school?" (I might hold something like that over my
children, too. Not only is money guilt but guilt is money in
the bank.) But I am confident that he would have done it,
and not only because my mother would have made him do
it. Do *something*.

My father was a solid, tithing, fund-raising Methodist.
But he had a Faustian streak, striving, demanding, delving
into the black arts of money breeding. He wouldn't have listened to the theory that money represents dung and the
devil (though that was the way Martin Luther felt), but if
Mephistopheles had come to my father with a plan to double Decatur Federal's assets, I think my father would have
heard him out with an eye toward finding some Methodist
adaptation of whatever asset-doubling strategy the devil had
in mind. My mother wouldn't have wanted to know about
it. She was pessimistic about worldly schemes. She was into
feeding, tending, fostering, teaching, and singing sadly
about the garden of prayer, not into overreaching.

The median salary for women in this country in 1982
was $131 a week lower than men's. One reason is
that women — for whatever tangled reasons of tradition,
psychology, physiology, and oppression — tend to have less
Faustian jobs than men. And Faustian is where the
money is.

Harrop points out in his book that all over the world — in

capitalist countries, communist countries, and countries too poor to be either one — mining workers make substantially more than agricultural workers. I'll tell you why: Mining is a more Faustian activity. Adam and Eve, before they were alienated, were small farmers. In modern economics, small farmers can't thrive (they are almost obsolete in this country; and in Russia, farm workers are the most dismally rewarded people in a nation of dismal rewards), because thriving is a matter of big numbers. Of biting off more than you can chew. Of doing something aggressive, alchemical, snaky, infernal, like capitalizing on the nest-building instinct or going underground after minerals that can be made to glitter or burn.

Of course nurses don't make serious money. They're in the tending-and-nourishing line. Money is for flashy, brazen work in Las Vegas — for wowing people who play games with chips of raw money.

I have forsaken Marxism, though. I could go for Marxism as long as it meant overthrowing a junta, but I don't want to *live under* it. Marx was right about capitalism's money fetish, but there is also such a thing as being obsessed with an ism. Marxism, in conflating morality and wherewithal, cuts no slack for those who disbelieve in Marxism or in economics or in whoever is in charge. In this country of checkered privilege — where you can make a nice dollar off of misery in crooked nursing homes or, less viciously and less cozily, by snatching gold chains from people's necks — you can sell copies of *The Communist Manifesto;* and if you can make a buck at it, capitalism has to hand it to you.

The problem with a just system of income is, who runs the Bureau of Economic Justice? According to Harrop's figures, the average book earns its author $2.29 an hour. My books, for instance, earn nurse's money compared with Judith Krantz's. But merit underrated, by the marketplace or by a bedlam of critics, still has more *bounce* to it than merit officially, ideologically defined. I think I would feel as stifled living in, say, Cuba as I would working for a major corporation.

What the world seems to be moving toward along various potholed routes (Reaganomics or no Reaganomics) is various forms of what I still say Marx should have resorted to: catch-as-catch-can synthesis of capitalism and socialism. Maybe it will dawn on the world how absurd and yet deep-seated salary structures are. Maybe somebody will come up with a Belushi Memorial Ism, whereby everybody can fatten unabashedly or else authentically sing the blues.

Under whatever system, each person eats a peculiar, hybrid knowledge-apple. I, for instance, inherited something of my father's streak and also my mother's feeling that it is no bargain. I am left with a taste not for salary, because salary lets you know exactly what you can and can't afford; and not for capital, because capital leads to Republicanism; but for producing a piece of writing (more or less as a self-fathering pig produces pork) that I enjoy, because I think it's worth something, in return for a piece of money that I enjoy, because I think it's worth something else.

By money I enjoy, I mean what characters in *Semi-Tough* call up-front whipout: money you spend. Spend it on pediatric medicine (including whatever it takes to finance the goddamn drug companies' lobby); spend it on barbecue; spend it on UNICEF and the ACLU; spend it on records and movies and books. Spend it on a savings-and-loan account, though that whole concept, I keep reading, is obsolete. (My father, may he strive in peace, also worked hard and well for Packard Motor Car Company and the Edsel; see Norman O. Brown on the notion of "a monument more enduring than bronze.") Spend it on staying out later than Faust.

Money, says a character in *Portrait of a Lady*, "is a terrible thing to follow but a charming thing to meet." Might as well acknowledge it the way you do death, guilt, magic, excreta, etcetera.

I'll tell you the honest truth: I don't know what I make.

Lord help me (if there is a heaven and I attain it, I'll share it with agricultural workers of Cameroun, who will take my lunch money every day), I just want to keep the feel of it in my pants.

BLUE YODEL 15

JUBAL

They picked me up at the home and took me to the Tennessee Wilson plays. This bunch of women did. At the Pistable Chutch. I never been in one before, a Pistable Chutch, I don't know who they wushup. My momma raised me Disciple of Christ. They drove nails in Jesus. If it was a Chutch of Bear Bryant, I might go to that.

They didn't drive nothin in Bear Bryant.

We seen two plays and sat around a circle and they give us each a Fig Newton. They said, "Mr. Oxgood, do you have any eractions to the plays you'd like to share?"

I said I didn't. They said why. I said, "It's hard for a crazy man to think."

They said, "Oh, Mr. Oxgood, don't say that!" So I took it out.

Genly they'll let me go on back to my room when I take it out.

They said, "Oh, Mr. Oxgood, put it back in!" But I got a good grip on it and held on.

But I lied about eractions. I had the eraction it was all crazy people in them plays. It wadn't but one person in them plays that anybody would spend fifteen minutes with if they dint haf to and that was that Gennleman Caller.

Deliver me from all them women in them plays.

There was one woman said, "I have always depended on the kindness of strangers." I ain't that crazy. I am crazy, but I ain't up for grabs.

Old Gennleman Caller broke the little glass horn off the unicorn. What use is a horn that breaks off? I'm crazy, but my horn ain't broke. Old Bobby Wheat over in Lampasas had one he could crack hickory nuts and loosen rusted-in bolts with. Called it old WD-40. "Giver a lick with old WD-40," us other boys on demolition'd say.

Them women probly dint know what WD-40 is. That means they don't get about half the remarks in this world.

The Secret of Gatorgate

IF the FBI would straight-out ask me whether I know who the so-called Debategate mole was, I would tell them. Yes, I know who the mole was. If "mole" is what you want to call a one-man, single-issue pressure group wearing an alligator costume.

But the FBI doesn't ask that. It asks whether I know anything about "a sexual videotape involving government officials."

Ironically enough, I tried to tell part of what I do know — and am about to reveal now — back in 1980. But editors then scoffed at the notion that Jimmy Carter had any kind of Francophile relative, much less one who would dress up like an alligator. Editors also accused me of bias.

I could see their point. For who stood to gain the most from the reelection of Jimmy Carter?

I did. My book Crackers — which explained, among many other things, the whole fascinating enigma of zero-based budgeting — appeared in September of that year. It was cannily timed to capitalize upon the Carter revival that was bound to coincide with his second, born-again, term of office. If Ronald Reagan were elected president, I feared, I would go on the "Today" show and be introduced by Tom Brokaw as "a man who has written a book that is already obsolete."

Now. Who stood to lose the most if Carter won?

The Ayatollah Khomeini. He was tired of keeping a lot of American hostages fed, on the one hand, and of keeping his most deeply inspired supporters from eating them, on the other. But he was damned if he was going to release them to Jimmy Carter, a Baptist.

Which leads us to Armand Carter, of Tchoupitoulas, Louisiana. A second cousin, twice removed, of the president, Armand Carter was obsessed with the threat of alligators to the French-poodle population of Louisiana.

"It gonna break you heart," he told me. "Too many alligators! Comin' up in people's yards. Gonna eat all the poodles! I gor-on-tee you!"

In what follows, I will no longer attempt to quote Armand verbatim. Cajun dialect, especially when muffled by an alligator costume, is hard to reproduce faithfully in print. Suffice it to say that Armand had been crawling back and forth in front of the White House gate in a costume depicting an alligator devouring a French poodle. Here is what happened to him, as he told it to me on the eve of the second Carter-Reagan debate:

Presidential aides had urged Jimmy Carter to have Armand locked up.

"He is my second cousin, twice removed," the president said, "and I love him."

"Let's just remove him one more time," the aides said, but the president held firm.

So the aides attempted to co-opt Armand. They ushered him into the White House. "Listen," they said to him, "what can we do to get you to stop crawling around the

White House in an alligator suit with a stuffed poodle in its mouth?"

All they could do, Armand insisted, was to take steps against alligator overpopulation, and concomitant poodle underpopulation, in Louisiana.

"We're busy trying to assure our reelection," the aides said. "But, tell you what. If you could do us a favor, one that would be of great value to the campaign, then we in turn, over the next four years, could do something for you on this alligator thing."

"What kind of favor?" Armand asked (in words to that effect).

"How'd you like to infiltrate the Reagan campaign and steal their debate briefing book?"

Armand wanted to know what a debate briefing book was.

"Like ours, here," the aides told him, and they showed him a loose-leaf notebook. All Armand could remember, later, of its contents was that if Reagan said, "There you go again," to Carter again, Carter planned to say, "I do not!"

Armand asked how he would go about infiltrating the Reagan campaign.

"You will have to disguise yourself as a Republican aide," the Carter aides said.

Just then a call came in from a Peruvian intermediary, and the Carter aides left Armand sitting there, seething. For one thing, it was hot inside his alligator-cum-poodle suit. For another thing, no American who is not in fact a Republican aide can imagine posing as one.

Armand was so angry that he picked up the Carter briefing book, stowed it in the zipper compartment in the poodle portion of his costume, and stalked — as well as a person so attired can stalk — out of the White House. Not wanting to deal directly with Republicans, he conveyed the briefing book to the ayatollah, who conveyed it to a man who (this is all I can say for certain) looked very much like William J. Casey.

The rest is history. I did go on the "Today" show. I was introduced by Tom Brokaw as "a man who has written a book that is already obsolete."

The Ayatollah Khomeini did release the hostages to Ronald Reagan, not a Baptist.

And now that this so-called Debategate flap has arisen, the third shoe has dropped. Unfortunately, Armand Carter's alligator suit was stolen from him — by Iranian agents, he believes — shortly after Reagan's election. And Armand Carter himself was stolen from my office last night.

At any rate, it was not Debategate, properly speaking. It was Gatorgate. And the mole inside the Carter campaign was not — all appearances aside — Jimmy Carter himself.

BLUE YODEL 16
LINC

I shouldn't tell this.

If a man goes to a druggist (did you ever see a woman druggist?) and says a certain thing, the druggist will look around to make sure no women are watching and then he will go over to a certain corner behind the counter and reach down low to the floor and push a certain button a certain number of short and long times in a certain order and a door will slide open. . . .

And there's something in there.

The druggist takes a tube of it out, looks around again to make sure no women are watching, and wraps it and slips it to the man.

Facial hair.

It's an ancient formula. It's a cream. A pilatory, is the technical term. You rub it into the pores. Every day about eight hours before shaving. Or, if you don't shave, add another layer the next day and it's cumulative. That's how we get whiskers. All of us.

You say, why bother? You say, who needs it? Well, why do you think grown-ups groan a lot and have bony feet and wrinkles? It's part of the mystique. It's so children will think being grown-up is hard.

You know sometimes men go off by themselves in the woods and get lost and never come back? Chances are they're the ones who forgot to take any cream with them.

If they've got their cream, they can keep on getting bristly, eating grubs, and looking for the highway. But after two days, no cream, and they're still lost and got no stubble, why, they do the honorable thing. Let a cougar eat them. Cougars pick up on the whole deal, by instinct. Evidently — I've never been in the situation — a cougar can just smell a man with no cream.

It doesn't work on heads.

Still in Remedial Bayoneting

WE now know, of course, that it is poppycock to assume that anything so simplistic and sexistically conceived as the H-Y antigen accounts for both the formation of testes and the tendency of female inbred mice to reject skin grafts from otherwise genetically identical males. Dr. Veva Labonne-Schaum, of the Einander Institute, discovered the fallacy of the H-Y hypothesis-hype when a colleague (myself) brought her, flippantly, two male mice that had given birth to tiny capsules of L'eggs hosiery.

Flippantly, because in those days I was in league with Dr. Chucky McArdle, whom I now see through.

"There are two subjects that should never be discussed in mixed company," McArdle would say. " 'Men,' and 'Women.' " That's the way he and I used to talk. We'd click our choppers at the giggly, halter-topped pipette girls ("lablollies," we called them), and cut our eyes over at our women colleagues and make cracks.

"No, three subjects," McArdle would go on. "Add 'Men and Women.' " In the first place, he would say, he could "argue till the . . . *cattle* come home" that he had put "Men" first for purely counterchivalric or alphabetical reasons, "and I would just be digging myself a deeper hole."

What he was saying implicitly, of course, was that *men* dig holes. I did dig a series of holes when I was nine, out in the side yard, for no reason except cultural compulsion. It was my father who fell into one of them and sent me away to military school, where I was forced to wear a shako and stand rigid for hours on end, but it was societal expectations that made me hack fruitlessly into the earth rather than aspire to the caring personhood of a John Derek, whose now-ex-wife Linda Evans has recalled: "It was the most wonderful life I can imagine any woman having. He would spend months handcrafting a vest or boots for me. Then he would wait for me to come home and have champagne and grapes individually dusted with sugar next to a fur bed he had laid by the fireplace."

McArdle and I never asked ourselves how a Derek managed to escape the traps this society lays for male children. McArdle maintained that Derek had been reared by Persian cats.

My father was a machinist. After grimly machining all one late-spring day and male-bonding into the night, he had slipped under cover of darkness into our side yard to plant a rhododendron — something green, something alive . . . One of my senseless excavations brought him down headlong on top of the flowering shrub in his arms. Its crushed white blossoms flushed with mauve clung to his Valvoline-ingrained skin. He screamed.

He had won the rhododendron in a poker game. But he had been touched by its beauty, and it tortured him to admit that, even to himself. For years afterward he clawed at those petals in his sleep, my mother later told me in (yes, a woman's) tears. When I was twelve — still in remedial bayoneting — my father left for Alaska and a life of oiling and rigging oil rigs and baiting Kodiak bears. We never again saw, as he would have put it, hide nor hair of him.

My father's and my emotions at the time of his accident went deep, but we didn't share them. My father screeched, for all the neighborhood to hear, when his role (as he must have seen it) was to bellow. That, I believe, was what caused him to pack me off. To Colonel Cobb's Weapons Pool and School: drill and ceremonies, drill and ceremonies, and grenade lobbing. It was not enough that we cadets be required to lob grenades. We had also, since they were duds brought back by Colonel Cobb from Tarawa, to make (our only aesthetic exercise) the sounds: "FOOOM-KA!" "H'WUMPF!" "BAROOOMP!" We loved it. So we told ourselves.

I stopped telling myself those things the day I, in totally the wrong spirit, brought Dr. Labonne-Schaum the *Freimäuse*.

It was McArdle who discovered the L'eggs capsules. It was I who brought them and the mice to her, on the assumption that she would be flustered, might even weep. It was she who, after fixing me with her litmus-blue eyes, perceived that the mice were not male but just, triumphantly, *Freimäuse*, or free mice.

I don't know whether it was the discovery or the look she gave me (in my mind, the two are inseparable), but at that moment my nature began to demand different things. McArdle had been wrong to call the *Freimäuse* "mice who've learned they can do any goddamn thing around this place and get attention." These were new mice. Mice who were ahead, in a real sense, of McArdle and me. Mice whose X *and* Y chromosomes had reoriented into the less binding W and Z.

And so: humanity will be able to start again from scratch. From a new scratch.

We have been feeling just as faded (in the sense of pallor, and in the sense that someone is betting against us) as our genes. We need fresh — clean — genes, and we can have them. The new genetics has already made major strides. (It was Major Matt Strides who shared Colonel Cobb's kampong. At night we could hear them bellowing.) We will be able by the end of the decade to be fitted in the womb *or a barber's chair* with the neutral W and Z, produced synthetically in pursuance of Dr. Labonne-Schaum's vision. The essential chromosomal material is a jelly (*Glück*), neither butch nor nellie, but simply rife. The rifeness is all.

I wish my father could be here to see what is coming. He lies in the ice, a mastodon. And Colonel Cobb died in the infamous Recoilless Rifle disco fire. History may forgive them. It will not forgive us, if we fail to grasp the new genetic moment.

Should there be two sexes? Should there be *only* two? The recombinance Dr. Labonne-Schaum projects would retain duality, but a duality reconceived. The two kinds of person would be "is" (*wasist*) and "err" (*istlos*). An err would embody the atom's flux, an is is its essentiality. An is would be into being, an err into wandering.

Would an err's sole domestic contribution then be "Honey, I'm home"? No. An is would depend for is (the possessive form, significantly, would be the same as the nominative) sense of being some*where* upon an err. An err would derive err sense of *having been* somewhere from an is.

Either without the other would be nowhere, hollow (*waslos*).

An is would have the mellower voice, an err reach more octaves. But either, on is or err own, could openly cherish a rhododendron. Either could be bushy-faced. If anyone felt like feeling like a frond, anyone could feel like one: a frond rooted (is) or a frond on the wind (err).

Would there be romance? How about periodic mutual dissolving dips into not just a pool but a gene lagoon? From which almost anything might emerge. Dripping. Sound kind of . . . mushy? Ah.

All of this opens up ahead of us now — thanks to a person the fine tracery of whose exhaustive research, the almost sensuous turn of whose thought, the permeating property of whose birdsong voice . . .

"That Chucky McArdle is a child. He put a rubber lipid in my retort."

. . . the fine beads of brow sweat, the lips full . . . chewy (she chews them) . . .

"Yesterday, he brought me coffee in one of those cups with the frog on the bottom."

. . . the kind of person, I tell her, who opens a person up, who causes a person's thinking to dip and dart . . .

"Of course you didn't notice. I wonder if you notice anything."

. . . who can make a person feel for a flash like a naked infant, feel for a flash like a naked woman must, feel like a bucket brigade.

"For a flash?"

She is *so* sharp, though, it sometimes seems a person can't say anything . . . Especially, it seems, when I am most open. Dr. Labonne-Schaum! *Ich bin keine Maus!*

BLUE YODEL 17

DARRELL

*There's this woman Mona I'm seeing, when I hold her
and squeeze her sometimes I think to myself: "Mona! I love
you so! You fill my heart until it overflows! I want to hold
you forever and squeeze you forever and love you with this
enormous passionate eternal feeling that comes over me
whenever I touch you like now! Lick you, roll you, extol
you, fold you, endlessly snuffle throughout and in and out
your sweet entire mellifluous utterly wa-wa-wa-woowoo —*
embrace *your being everandevermoreafter with all of my
burgeoning might!"*

*And just when I can't hold it in anymore I bust out with
". . . might!" and find myself adding, ". . . be a good idea if
we went to the 6:55 show so we don't have to wait in line."*

*I don't tell her any of that other stuff! Something stops
me!*

I'll tell you what it is.

I don't want to give her the wrong idea.

"I Always Plead Guilty"

Fucking up is not what it used to be. Sure, there are plenty
of people around these days whom you could call fuck-ups;
but I'm talking about celebrative, life-enhancing, go-get-'em
fucking up, a traditional male imperative. There used to be

politicians like Big Jim Folsom, governor of Alabama in the late forties and the early fifties. Folsom was a liberal redneck who snorted at segregationist blowhards, drank with Adam Clayton Powell, and once fell out of the gubernatorial jeep while inspecting ROTC troops at the University of Alabama. Would you vote for a man who would inspect ROTC troops sober? When accused of involvement with an attractive blond not his wife, he said the whole thing was political, and if his enemies were going to stoop to using such bait, "they're going to catch Big Jim every time." Many another indiscretion was laid at his doorstep, and he said: "I plead guilty. I always plead guilty. Now, why don't we get on with the issues here?"

Big Jim's career ended when he went on television during a reelection campaign, began to introduce his family, and affectionately forgot all of his children's names. "He was a combination of genius, moron and alcoholic," said a supporter, "and the thing that made it exciting was that each morning when he woke up, you never knew which one it was going to be."

America was built on unpredictable combinations. Big Jim fucked up *royally* — and generously. People still tell stories about him with pleasure.

Today, across the land, that kind of thing is down the drain. A thin, self-serving Republican order prevails, and it is hard even to see any potential great fuck-ups on the horizon. Prince Andrew? He's *British*. Francis Ford Coppola? He created an idiosyncratic, overextended Hollywood studio, to be sure, but it produced some extraordinarily underextended movies — as if Napoleon had marched his armies into Russia in order to seize the "Style" section of *Pravda*.

How did this country's great fuck-up tradition become so attenuated?

I blame the economy. "There are men in the world," said Winston Churchill, who was one of them, "who derive as stern an exaltation from the proximity of disaster and ruin as others from success." But who can afford disaster and ruin today? The stakes are too high, because of inflation, and it's too hard to bounce back, because of recession. Outfits that venture greatly today rely so heavily on market research that it doesn't matter, except in terms of money, whether they succeed or not. For an individual to survive today, he just about has to work for a corporation. How can you fuck up with any flair for a corporation?

I blame cocaine. The state-of-the-art fuck-up fuel is too expensive and dangerous. People don't fuck up *amiably* on, or in connection with, cocaine. Look what it's done to sports, Hollywood, and John DeLorean. Most people I know have stopped trying to keep up with getting high. Many of them have stopped drinking — even stopped eating meat. You can't fuck up on tofu.

I blame the legal profession. When a caveman fucked up, he would whang and wiggle his way out of it, fucking up further in the process and learning new lessons for himself. And the community would learn from his example: "Well, boys, I guess it ain't a good idea to try cooking a live mastodon so close to the house. Glad I got to see it, though." When a person fucks up today, it means raising $300,000 for the lawyers. Then you get thrown in jail, anyway, with a bunch of crazy fuckers who couldn't afford lawyers and have been lifting weights for fifteen years. And your lawyers say: "Well, we fucked up. Interesting case, though." The lawyers get all the fun. And the only thing the community learns is not to get out of line.

I blame the Reagan administration. Have you ever seen *The Killers,* Ronald Reagan's last movie (presumably)? He plays the kingpin crook, prune-faced and prim-lipped but with a certain calm presence. It appears that what he is doing — even when he is knocking Angie Dickinson flat with a right hand — is clear in his own mind. And yet everybody in the movie is constantly fucking up. John Cassavetes keeps letting Angie fuck him up, Reagan fails to shoot either Cassavetes or Lee Marvin completely dead, and, in the end, everybody dies and the money blows away. But, hey, crooks in movies are *supposed* to fuck up. John, Lee, and Angie get a bang out of the screwing and the shooting, but Ron doesn't. When he reaches the end of the line, he looks at the wad of cash that has entangled him in all this human sloppiness, and he shakes his head irritably. In this, his last movie scene, you can see him thinking: "I am tired of this business. There are bound to be easier ways to make a lot of money. I believe I will become president . . . of a land where major corporations are in charge and there is absolutely no charm left in fucking up."

One way to keep fucking up down is to keep unemployment up. Every person who is out of work is one fewer person who finds stories of fucking up on the job entertaining. People nowadays are either looking for security or trying to keep it. In the sixties, college students tried to fuck up the system. Today college students are afraid they'll fuck up and not find a slot in it.

If you stay in a slot, there are things you never learn. Fucking up brings people into contact with the world's actual contours and forces, as in "I fought the law and the law won." Unemployment does the same thing but with no thrill involved. When you're fucking up, you know you're not just coasting along and losing momentum. You're *venturously* finding out what you can't get away with. The difference between fucking up and being unemployed is the difference between tackling a lion and being gnawed on by one. There just might be a way that tackling a lion would work. If nobody ever fucked up, how would human progress be made? I once heard it said of a straitlaced, cautious man that "he don't know anything, because he's never done anything *wrong.*"

Fucking up is part of heroism. It entails leaping to conclusions. King Lear and Oedipus spring to mind. The hero is always primed for situations in which most people would be moved to shut their eyes tight and say, "Ohhhhhhh, shit!" Heroes come through frequently, fuck up often, sometimes do both at once. Fucking up is trying things that probably won't work, just in case they will and because, at any rate, they bring adrenaline.

The great writers — Shakespeare, Balzac, Tolstoy, Dickens, Twain — are not those who never depart from elegance but those who can be awful and who tend to fuck up largely in life as well as in art. Fucking up comes from going into the unknown for the challenge of it and is, thus, a very American thing. "We are all Americans at puberty," said Evelyn Waugh, and puberty is prime fuck-up time. Europeans don't fuck up or venture as greatly as Americans (they used to, back when they were discovering and fucking up the New World).

Fucking up also comes from doing things that deep down inside you know better than. America has had the requisite mixture of innocence, which gets you into trouble, and conscience, which makes you recognize that you are in it. Russia is too innocent to fuck up — innocent in the sense of lacking qualms. Vietnam was a fuck-up, but invading Afghanistan wasn't. Two-thirds of the American consciousness was saying, "This seems like the thing to do; what the hell," and another two-thirds was saying, "This is a horrible thing to do," and the overlap started out saying, "We are doing this only for the sake of those poor peasants" but finally swung around to "Well, we have fucked up." Russia's values aren't complicated enough for fucking up. Russia calculates and moves, and if the move turns out to be too costly, the national calculation is adjusted; historical inevitability prevails throughout. The Reagan administration's values are also uncomplicated.

Democrats fuck up more than Republicans, with the exception of Nixon — an unusual Republican in that he wanted to do new things and in that he gave (instead of just calling) new things a bad name. Coolidge, for all of his passive contributions to the Depression, didn't fuck up; LBJ, a man of boom and bathos, did. Franklin Roosevelt fucked up the system enough to save it; there was something wicked in his grin that made him believable. Since Nixon, no president has been able to get away with an up-to-something look. Carter tried to take bold steps and yet assure everyone of the essential sweetness and rationality of them; fucking up and Sunday school don't mix.

The Reagan administration doesn't fuck up. When we learn that the Environmental Protection Agency has been sucking up to chemical companies, our reaction is, "Well, of course." That, by the Reagan administration's standards, is the EPA's *mission*. (Similarly, the Department of the Interior's current role is to spread the interior's legs.) Here is the kind of goal that the Reagan administration has: To put more money into the arms race. How can you fuck that up? It's like letting the water out of a tub. A child could do it. Another thing the Reagan administration is keen on is saying nasty things about Russia. Anybody in the world can think of nasty things to say about Russia. What takes imagination is thinking of things to say about Russia that aren't nasty and yet make sense. Still another trick the Reagan administration has managed to pull off is to make the rich get richer and the poor get poorer. If the Reagan administration were a refrigerator, it would say that its purpose was to let ice melt. And people wonder how the president manages to stay so relaxed.

It's almost enough to make a man feel depressed. Recently, I heard a woman author tell an audience that men know nothing about friendship because they never have lunch together to tell each other how depressed they are. Well, "depressed" may be a word that women feel more comfortable with than men do. Men don't generally like to say they're depressed, not in so many words. I think you have to give men some credit for that, because there are no more boring — not to say depressing — words in English than "I am depressed." That's one of the shortcomings of *being* depressed.

Men would rather have lunch together to tell each other how badly they have fucked up. But I like to be progressive when it comes to male-female roles, so the other day, at lunch, I said I was depressed. My friend Fletch said, "Well, don't feel pregnant," and my friend Kirby said, "Join the fucking club."

"I knew a guy was so depressed once," my friend Chet put in, "that he took his bowling ball and swung it into his TV screen, and when it stuck there, he dragged the whole thing to the window and dropped it onto the top of his car, where it stuck. Then he went outside and drove his car into his picture window, where *it* stuck. Then he climbed up on top of his car, put his fingers in the bowling-ball holes and now he had a grip on everything he owned, except for his catfish pond. So he tried to roll it all down the hill into his catfish pond. But, of course, it wouldn't budge. So then he went down to the pond and dynamited all the fish and loaded them into garbage bags and dragged them up the hill and put them in his car and then he rented himself a pump and —"

"Kiss my ass if that ain't depressed," said my friend the Dipper.

"I knew an old boy was so depressed, he took a wood-splitting maul and busted every toilet in the house into chunks and threw them at the police car when it came," mused Kirby.

"Shit, you call that depressed?" exclaimed Chet. "I remember a time —"

"If that was all he owned, how'd he round up all the dead fish?" interrupted Fletch. "He must have owned a boat."

"I'd like to get me one of those overland car-boats," said the Dipper. "A man had one of those, he could just *take off*. Any direction."

"Who makes one of those?" asked Fletch.

"What do you want to know for?" I asked. "You'd just run it off a cliff."

"Do they make one that flies?" asked the Dipper.

I'm not saying that busting up all your toilets is a good idea. But I can see how it might be more gratifying to a man than seeking sympathy for being depressed. It wouldn't be gratifying worth a damn to anybody else in the house, especially anybody who was looking forward to a few minutes of quiet bathroom relaxation, but at least it would keep people busy, stimulate the economy. What the male midlife crisis amounts to, probably, is a man's heaving and thrashing against having to admit to himself that he knows what depression means. When a man gets depressed, it's doubly depressing, because he knows he's not supposed to get depressed at all. He's supposed to be out vigorously fucking up. Women blues singers voluptuate in the blues more than men blues singers, who are more likely to sound like they are keeping one eye and a couple of incisors up out of the feeling.

There is a difference between "I have fucked up" and "I am fucked up." There was a time when a man might enjoy using "Boy, am I fucked up!" as a dope-and-liquor reference, because that meant he had fucked himself up. It was something he had *done*. A man feels obliged to represent himself as having *acted*, even if only upon himself. Lately, however, self-intoxication is also not what it used to be.

Willie Nelson sings, convincingly, about how he's "gotta get drunk" and, unconvincingly, about how he sure does dread it. So, once, did many country singers carry on. Now Hank Williams, Jr., sings "All My Rowdy Friends Have Settled Down." Richard Burton has quit drinking. So has Billy Carter. America is in a sober period — fucking up is not reinforced by the culture. Famous people do sit-ups and curry their investments rather than raise hell and explore the forbidden. It got to the point, I guess, that the only forbidden things left were things that only a complete damn fool would do. But does that mean we have to put our energy into aerobics?

It seems only yesterday that going out on a limb for an unstable convict with a dark view of the underside was exactly what serious people were *supposed* to do. When Norman Mailer — long a fuck-up genius — did it for Jack Henry Abbott and Abbott killed a man, it was a fuck-up that multitudes leaped to denounce and disparage. Multitudes applaud when Ronald Reagan speaks of locking people up and throwing away the key. Doesn't anybody remember when multitudes thought that there might be a sense in which criminals held a key — a key to evil, to sheer freedom? Remember when the culture wanted to delve into evil, into anarchy? Now it doesn't. Now it wants to see movies about the Force, Gandhi, and sweet-natured E.T., who tells the granddaughter of John Barrymore (talk about a guy who could fuck up!) to "be good." Or else movies like *Trading Places* and *Risky Business,* in which young heroes learn how to make good by fitting groovily into corruption.

Famous athletes used to fuck up extravagantly, entertainingly. The team would be huddled in pregame locker-room prayer and somebody would look up and Joe Don Looney would be dancing the mashed potatoes. Tim Rossovitch would open his mouth in a fraternity meeting and a live bird would fly out. Now athletes either carry briefcases or get into grim trouble over drugs or both. I don't mean to suggest that I am in favor of drinking problems or that I don't take them seriously. But hasn't there been an amazing rash of *reformed* alcoholism in sports today? When Neil Allen was pitching for the Mets, he announced that he had a drinking problem, and the team doctors said no, he didn't. The first case of hysterical alcoholism I ever heard of.

Sure, you have sports figures misbehaving today. John McEnroe pouts and snarls and curses at tennis judges twice his age, on television, and gets his wrist slapped occasionally, and makes $75,000 a night for exhibitions. George Steinbrenner hires and fires Billy Martin over and over in a numbing drama of subordination and insubordination. That kind of thing is not fucking up. That kind of thing is jerking off.

There doesn't seem to be any real *heart* to public fucking up today. When was the last time anybody did anything outrageous that was also funny? Or even stimulating? When Richard Pryor fucked up free-basing, he found that "when you run down the street on fire, people get out of your way." But his act also got a bit too mellow in spots. And he looked miserable on Oscar night, reading an unfunny, industry-prepared script. You hear people say now that Richard Pryor is yesterday's great black comedian, Eddie Murphy is today's. Eddie Murphy is upscale. He is on top of things. But he has yet to produce the kind of desperate, rallying exhilaration that Pryor snatched out of deep, beat-down, fucked-up blues.

Is there any bohemia anymore? Are there any crazy-poet, piss-in-the-fireplace characters like Maxwell Bodenheim? I'm not saying such characters are necessarily good poets. I'm saying we need such characters in the arts. To live in Greenwich Village or SoHo today, you've got to have two accountants. Artists are big businessmen. Remember when the pop-cultural scene was Jack Nicholson and the "Saturday Night Live" guys and Hunter Thompson and Kris Kristoffersen and various British actor-rounders carousing? I guess John Belushi ran self-destructiveness into the ground. Belushi was a hell of a guy. What would a guy like that be doing speedballs for? He must have been kind of fucked up. That's chilling.

A man does not want to say, "Boy, am I fucked up!" to mean that there is something deeply wrong with him psychologically. Especially if there is. You never hear John

Hinckley, Jr., for instance, say, "Am I fucked up!" Why you ever hear John Hinckley, Jr., say anything is beyond me; but, at any rate, your basic assassin-nebbish is driven to fuck up, big, so he won't have to admit that he is just, ingloriously, fucked up.

When you say, "I *am* fucked up," the person you are talking to feels called upon to say, "Oh, no you're not," in a nice way. Men resist saying such mollifying things to each other, because "mollifying" has "Molly" in it. Men like to say things like "roger wilco" and "Jack Daniel's." Men may enjoy accusing each other of being fucked up, in an obliquely complimentary way, but they would rather hear each other say, "Boy, have I ever fucked up!" because then they know a story is coming.

For instance: "I wake up all of a sudden and jump off the train, and I'm already in the parking lot before I realize that Jo Beth and the kids were riding with me, and they were asleep, too, and they are probably now halfway to Wilmington, Delaware. I figure, I'm this close to the car, I'll go ahead and get a drink somewhere and figure out how to track them down. So I jump into the Firebird —"

"You've got a new car?"

"Yep. Wrote a check for the whole thing. Had $320 in the bank. And I owe $19,000 in back taxes. If somebody calls you looking for me and you hear banking or IRS noises in the background, don't tell him anything. Anyway, I figure I'll have a couple of pops and think about the train thing, because I remember Jo Beth doesn't have any money with her, because I took the cash out of her pocketbook after she went to sleep because I was a little short.

"Fortunately, I get stopped for going ninety-five on the beltway on my way *to* the bar. But when I give the cop my license, I ask him whether he can't read it a little faster, because I'm in a hurry to get a drink — which is not a good move, because it turns out my license is expired and he gives me some shit and I'm not in the *mood* for it, so I give *him* some shit, and the next thing I know, he's got me out with my hands on top of the car, frisking me, and he finds this illicit substance my lawyer's wife gave me and one thing leads to another and I'm running down the median strip, you know, and I hear warning shots and the whole deal.

"So I run down the on-ramp there, where it comes in from Turlbut Boulevard, and jump down and grab a light stanchion and climb down onto the lower level and hitch a ride with this Italian woman Donna in a leopard-skin van who takes me to this joint where I use the phone to call my lawyer, figuring I might have some legal problems, but when I get to the part about the illicit substance, he says, 'Where'd you get that?' And I say, 'This broad I'm seeing, Ceci—,' about to say, 'Cecily gave it to me,' but then it hits me Cecily is his wife and there's this awkward pause — I should've said 'Cecilia' or something right quick, but I had so much on my mind — and he hangs up on me. I think I've really fucked up this time."

Well, that kind of story doesn't go over as well as it used to. For one thing, people have come to realize that it is no wonder that Jo Beth and Donna and Cecily are depressed.

Why is it that I think of fucking up, in the flamboyant, exploratory sense, as mostly a male thing? It may be because women have that nicely balanced XX chromosome whereas men have that wild-hair XY. Or it may just be because men have traditionally had more opportunity to fuck up. Women traditionally have been home taking care of hearth and kiddies so men could have the latitude to fuck up. When you fuck up in the oil business, it's kind of exciting and you can start over. When you fuck up raising children, it's just bad. One way women have been kept in their traditional place is that when women fuck up, men don't slap them on the back. Men fuck up; women go wrong.

That is changing. But modern women who take control of their own lives and so on aren't interested in fucking up.

They are interested in proving that they can run a tight-ship software firm. They are looking for twenty-year-old guys with nice pecs to have some fun with, and then for stable mates who do housework and can keep track of their own socks. One thing women are definitely not interested in is becoming characters in men's fuck-up stories.

I also think there is a deep feeling in the land that nobody wants to be a character in a Ronald Reagan fuck-up story.

Personally, I think that the president's great gift is for seeming to be less out-to-lunch than he looks. He can play unruffledness well. And we feel that we have a stake in keeping him unruffled, because if he ever decides that being president is as messy a business as crime was in *The Killers*, he is also likely to decide that the whole world would be better off in heaven.

Reagan is very good at putting himself on the side of the angels. Whereas the patron saint of fucking up is Satan. Satan started out as an angel. But was he satisfied? No. He rebelled against the Almighty and, according to *Paradise Lost*, got himself

> *Hurled headlong flaming from th' ethereal sky*
> *With hideous ruin and combustion down*
> *To bottomless perdition, there to dwell*
> *In adamantine chains and penal fire.*

"Headlong flaming." All right! It sounds so much more bracing than sitting around with nuns and Albert Schweitzer playing harps. Maybe nuns are completely different in heaven, but I wouldn't count on it. And Schweitzer is probably lost in hard-to-share nostalgias.

"You want to play some *hoops* for a change?" you ask Schweitzer, and he just mumbles, "*Ach*" — not because in heaven the ball always goes in but because what he really wants is to be down putting poultices on the damned. And, hey, you've got to respect the guy. You've got to respect the nuns, too.

I seem to have written myself very nearly into an identification with the Prince of Darkness. (Milton did the same thing in *Paradise Lost*.) I want to back off from that. "Sympathy for the Devil" was a callow song (especially at Altamont, when the Rolling Stones were singing it while somebody was being stabbed to death by Hell's Angels). People who actually enter hell, prison, an asylum, the courts, or delirium tremens invariably report that either heaven or workaday life is gravely preferable. I'll take their word for it. But isn't there some middle ground? Why do we have to draw back so *far* from the abyss?

Well, we've got this Nuclear Shadow problem. Not a devil-may-care issue. Let some general fuck up with the buttons and . . . Vietnam was coupled with antiwar high-jinks and consciousness expansion, Watergate with dashing journalism. People don't get psyched up when they contemplate the fucking up of the universe as a whole.

But, hey, come on. Nature's little building block is a wild and crazy thing. All those quarks and mesons bounding around. Here's the Ultimate Fuck-up story: Morning after the world exploded, right? Millions of souls, in no mood for levity, stand at one gate or the other. Saint Peter (vexed) and the devil (impressed, in spite of himself) exclaim simultaneously to the multitudes: "You people are really something! Who'd've thought you'd fuck up the *atom*?"

The Creator, hovering over the new void, intones:

OH, IT FIGURED.
I PROBABLY SHOULD HAVE USED SOMETHING A LITTLE SMALLER.
MAYBE I'LL WRAP IT A LITTLE TIGHTER NEXT TIME.
OR LOOSER.
BUT THERE'S ALWAYS GOING TO BE A LITTLE KICKER IN THERE.

BLUE YODEL 18
MARV AND GEORGE

MARV: *When April cried my first reaction would be: "Oh, Jesus! She must feel as miserable as I would feel if I cried like that." I knew better. It's like a woman thinking, "Oh, Jesus, he must be as much in love as I would be if I were as turned on as he is." But I couldn't help it. That was my reaction. And it made me feel miserable. And then I would think: "Why should I feel so miserable? She may not even feel this miserable. What can I have done to make her feel this miserable?"*

GEORGE: *Yeah. But you can't say to a woman, "Hey, how can I be that bad a guy?" It's like saying, "Hey, you know, I'm a Christian, after all," to an Iranian fanatic.*

MARV: *Women don't know what they do to people when they cry. It's what they have instead of violence.*

GEORGE: *That's right. Tears are their terrorism. Let's face it, women are the Third World.*

MARV: *I never understand it when women say men should cry more. If men could cry like April and had upper-body strength . . . Not that I ever hit April. At all.*

GEORGE: *It's like the United States and the Lebanese. Can't make 'em happy, can't use our might on 'em.*

MARV: *Actually, the unselfish thing probably would have been if I had hit her. Not hard. It would have clarified the issues for her. But who am I, Santa Claus?*

GEORGE: *Action. When you're an exploited people, you like action. Because it's never your fault.*

MARV: *April hit me once. When she was crying. I held her arms. It just happened once. She could see it strengthened my position.*

GEORGE: *Like if Cuban ground troops invaded Miami and the U.S. hardly even noticed.*

MARV: *Crying was her real threat. It was like the earth opening up. Indisputable.*

GEORGE: *The powerless are always right.*

MARV: *I should've been able to do something. But . . . I wasn't on the right moral level. Whatever I did would've been either more of the same or capitulation, which was also no good to her.*

GEORGE: *Whether by tyranny or revolution, the people are always betrayed.*

MARV: *When women talk about men learning to cry, I think they have in mind some kind of soft, supportive crying. Sympathetic crying. I don't think they want men to cry like April did.*

GEORGE: *Any more than Libya really wants the U.S. economy to collapse.*

MARV: *I said, "Let's talk it out." She said: "That's not fair. You've got that big deep voice." I said: "Well god damn! I've got a big deep voice, you've got —" I didn't know exactly what I was going to say then, but I knew that whatever it was, I better not say it.*

GEORGE: *The Third World can say whatever pops into its head about Uncle Sam. Uncle Sam must bite his tongue.*

MARV: *So, if I couldn't assume that April felt as miserable as I would feel if I were crying like that, what could I assume?*

GEORGE: *America, unlike former imperial powers, cannot in character assume: "That's just wogs. Too quick to feel oppressed. Needn't read too much into it."*

MARV: *But I didn't know what the differential was, between how miserable I would feel if I ever cried like that and how miserable she actually felt. Science ought to develop a way to measure misery waves.*

GEORGE: *Back during Vietnam, it seemed like every woman I got involved with was either an ARVN or a Viet Cong. Which by definition, either way, was my fault.*

MARV: *Sometimes I think women cry over things that would just make men say, "Well, shit."*

GEORGE: *Except there was this one who was like China. Hard-core anti-running-dog China, before normalized relations. Profound, but always convulsed. And I'm saying, "Well, gee . . ."*

MARV: *There's got to be some common denominator. Men and women are not apples and oranges.*

GEORGE: *Why do I always have to be America? I'd like to be Kuwait for a couple of weeks. Then Antigua.*

MARV: *I talked to April's psychiatrist. He explained that she felt overpowered by me because I was so objective. I should lose my temper, he said. I talked to April about it. She said he was right. So the next time she cried, I yelled and flung my arms and jumped up and down and got incoherent. It did me a lot of good. You know what she said? "I thought I could at least count on you to be objective."*

GEORGE: *Or if I've got to be America, then why can't I be involved with, I don't know. Mexico? Sweden? I'll take Switzerland for a secretary and be in love with . . . I ought to say a major power. But there aren't any really friendly major powers.*

MARV: *I wonder whether Nancy Reagan ever cries.*

GEORGE: *Big Ron knows how to handle that. Waltz straight out the door and pick up a quick Grenada.*

MARV: *Yeah. Sometimes I envy conservatives.*

Out of the Clauset

LAST Christmas someone asked if I would play Santa Claus for his children and their friends. Actually dress up in a full Santa suit that he would rent.

I said no.

He was taken aback. He couldn't understand why I would pass up such a heartwarming opportunity. Kids regarding me with eyes of wonder. Eyes of "Wonder who put this total donut-hole up to this?" is more like it, I said.

I remembered how my friend Dupree Culp felt when he portrayed Santa back in college, at a party our fraternity gave for local orphans. We needed a community-service credit to offset what had happened when one of the brothers, Brince Ealey, regained unconsciousness unexpectedly one Sunday morning in the shrubbery outside Grace Boulevard Methodist Church. Unable to place himself at all, Brince perceived a world blotted out by a mass of tiny leaves except for a series of pastel-colored high-heel shoes, which were crunching in the pea-gravel walkway past his face. In a kind of paroxysm, he ruined a lot of hedge, tore off one whole leg of his bermuda shorts, and upended three prominent Methodist women.

This is by no means characteristic of Brince Ealey today. He is a congressman and outspoken foe of governmental action, who recently — after his eight-year-old daughter came home from school with the idea that Latin American people don't believe in Uncle Sam — proposed that "reinforcement of American belief" be mandated through twelfth grade at least.

Dupree Culp had always associated Santa with the triggering of innocent ecstasy. In his childhood — thanks to his mother, who had been orphaned, first by an oil stove and then by a locomotive, just before the Depression — Christmas morning was something precisely commensurate with his capacity for wonder. "Even when I didn't get the Erector Set I asked for one year," he told me, "I figured if I didn't get it, I must not have really wanted it."

Dupree said his mother often told him that she treasured nothing in this world the way she treasured seeing the expression on his face every Christmas morning when he saw what lay under the tree. *Plenty*. From out of the blue.

And Dupree said he didn't feel obliged to have a certain expression, either. He had it naturally. Every year, his mother would suggest how good of him it would be if he set aside one of his presents to give to some poor child through the church, and he always agreed and felt good about the idea, but she never actually made him do it.

So Dupree jumped at playing Santa Claus. The first jarring note came as he got into his suit. I was watching him. Everything in the costume worked except the hat.

We take a great many things for granted in this country, until we find ourselves responsible for bringing them off. Santa Claus's hat is a good example. Dupree wore his hair short, as was the fashion in 1961, and the hat wouldn't sit up on his head. It flopped down over his eyes and onto his chin. The pompon bounced around on his face when he walked or tried a "*Ho-ho-ho.*"

When he moved the pompon to the back, the hat looked like a red skullcap. When he draped the pompon to one side, he appeared to be wearing the headdress of a fey Turkish pirate. Dupree was upset. He wanted to be convincing. At my suggestion, he gave the hat some body by stuffing it with cotton. "It looks like a sundae," he complained. But after we pinned more cotton around the edges to represent snowy hair, the effect was pretty good. The hat/hair ensemble tended to stay in one place, which meant it changed position relative to his head when he made sudden movements, but he said he wouldn't make any more sudden movements.

The doorbell rang, heralding the orphans. Dupree took his bag of gifts and crawled composedly up into the chimney.

Actually, there was no chimney. We had a false fireplace in the fraternity house. But it was a big one, and for some reason it extended upward, above the level of the mantel, into a dark pocket somewhat larger than Dupree. He climbed into this hidden space, with his bag on his shoulder, and hung there, completely out of sight.

In the entrance hall, the orphans were given lime sherbet melting in ginger ale. Then they were ushered into the large common room where the fireplace was. The orphans milled about. They sipped or spilled their punch. They looked around. Dupree was building suspense.

There was a soft plop. The orphans turned, as one orphan, toward the fireplace. There, like a small, dead, red-and-white animal on a white nest, sat Dupree's hat and snowy hair. Dupree explained later that he had felt something "trying to fly" deep in his ear. "It didn't seem to want to come out," he said. "It seemed to want to get further in." For the orphans' sake, Dupree had hung there stoically. But he had tried to nudge his ear with his shoulder, and in so doing had dislodged his headpiece. When the orphans saw it fall, they flocked to the hearth and peered up at him.

Dupree hung there, jouncing his head awkwardly and trying to think. The orphans said things like "Right. Sure." He had lost the element of surprise.

There was no turning back. Dupree dropped into the children's midst, reclaimed his hat and hair from one of them, jumped up and down on one foot like someone with water on the ear, and put his hat and hair back on. "Ho-ho-ho," he said.

There is nothing quite so flat as a "Ho-ho-ho" that has a distracted and also a resigned quality. By this time, the moth or whatever it was had left, but you know how you feel when something strange has just been in your ear. Dupree focused on the children's faces, but their expressions were not what he had had in mind.

Perhaps he should have shown what today's trend-setters call attitude, and said: "Okay. We all know there is no Santa Claus." But what if one of the orphans had *not* known? How would that child have felt, finding out from Santa Claus himself?

As Dupree handed out presents, one of the orphans slipped past him to look up into the fireplace again. Dupree grabbed at him, but he got by.

"Hey," the orphan said. "No hole in the top. How'd you get *in*? Hunh?" His "Hunh?" was hearty.

Then Brince Ealey woke up under a big sofa across the room and began sneezing and throwing up through his nose simultaneously, a terrible sound. As the children moved in that direction, Dupree took his empty bag and left.

He declined the role of Father Christmas the following year. That was when the orphans, having had four parties already that week and being due at another one in less than an hour, forced their way into the room where Santa — Brince Ealey — was getting into his suit.

The orphans found Brince in his beard, his red pants, and a fuzzy blue cardigan sweater. Most people in that situation would have felt like Venus observed while trying to find something under a chest of drawers, but in those days Brince could go with nearly anything, as long as, frankly, he hadn't passed out yet. Brince yelled, "Christmas is over! Easter time!" and led the orphans down to the kitchen, where they broke five dozen eggs. It was not until the fourth semester of his junior year that Brince did a complete 180: stopped raising hell, became a straight arrow, and ran for Honor Council.

Dupree felt strongly that Brince, in his partying days, was the wrong person to be Santa Claus. "I'm probably responsible," he said, "for letting the orphans' party fall off to the point where it would even occur to anyone that Brince Ealey should play Santa."

"But you meant well," I told him. "You could have just strolled in through the door and been cool. You got in the chimney because you wanted to suspend disbelief."

"My mother *did* suspend it," he said. He's career-Army now, intelligence. The last time I saw him, he couldn't tell me what he was doing, except that he was authorized to carry a pistol on commercial flights.

Let's face it. In any period of history, being Santa Claus requires craft, timing, good breaks, and a specially constructed hat. Nobody wants a clown for a benefactor. (These days, nobody wants a benefactor at all. Everyone wants to feel that whatever he has he took.) Santa must be generosity personified, but also self-preserving. A fine line there.

Particularly today! Contemporary American children, if they are old enough to grasp the concept of Santa Claus by Thanksgiving, are able to see through it by December 15. In the movie *Trading Places*, which has found favor with the make-or-break youth audience, Dan Aykroyd eats a stolen smoked salmon through the beard of his Santa costume, on the subway, drunk. Beard and fish become horribly entwined. When I saw that scene, a child sitting near me exclaimed, "Ewwwww, *yuck!*" Her eyes were shining.

However, I don't think we need to assume that the death of innocence is set in concrete. Things change. Brince Ealey changed. His daddy made him.

I Didn't Do It

BLUE YODEL 19
TWO MEN IN CENTRAL PARK

They are waiting for a free performance of *Coriolanus* to begin. The first speaker is maybe sixty, and has just sat back down after yelling to someone with a portable radio three rows back: "Impertinent! Impertinent! Should I beat a drum? I'll beat a drum, he blow a flute, you play jatz on the radio." The second is about forty, and is wearing a red tam.

"*That is not the class I come here to meet.*"

"*You meet a different class here.*"

"*Higher.*"

"*Yeh, higher, more intelligent than you meet on the subway.*"

"*You ever been to Cannes?*"

"*Cannes, France, yeah. Barcelona . . .*"

"*You read Doity Hands?*"

"*It's wonderful isn't it, about Communism.*"

"*Anyway, you are intelligent.*"

"*I sometimes wish I was, but I don't know whether I am. I don't get to have enough conversation.*"

"*You are not married?*"

"*I would have to like a person more. If a girl had a million dollars, and was beautiful, and I just liked her a little, I wouldn't marry her.*"

"*Yes.*"

"*Some couples are intellectually incompatible. I've known cases of that. Say a guy is stupid, and his wife tells him to go to school, to improve himself. And he gets mad, and she yells at him, and he beats her, and there are children."*

"Yes."

"Are you married?"

"I've got troubles enough. Should I make unhappy somebody else just because we've got something in common?"

"If more people thought like you did there'd be less divorces."

"That's why there are so many divorces."

The List of the Mohicans [1]

WHEN I sit down and make up a list of the things I will do today, I never do any of them. That is not to say I don't do anything. I may compose an operetta. But I don't do any of the things on the list.

And what am I going to do with an operetta? I don't know any violinists. Violinists may not be the first thing that springs to mind in connection with an operetta, but someone has to think of them at some point. Now that I have an operetta, I've got to sit down and make a list:

1. See about staging of operetta.
   a. Union difficulties?
   b. Real horses?
   (1) Check legality.

Lists generate sublists. And now that I have an item 1.b.(1), I have to have a 1.b.(2). I learned this in school. I may not need a 1.b.(2), but I have to have one. I also have to have an item 2. Now who is in charge, me or the list?

1. a. Chingachgook.
   b. Porthos?
   c. Uncas.

That is the question. When I am making a list, I feel dynamic, goal-oriented, ahead of the game. When the list is finished and I am looking at it, the power has shifted. I have to do what the list says.

But even while making the list, I am subject to certain laws:

1. Plurality.
    a. You can't have a list that says just "1. Be Thyself."
    b. You have to have a list that says
        (1) For instance, "1. Be Thyself"
        (2) And something else, like "2. Think About It."
    c. And then you are in trouble.
        (1) Because how can you be *being* something — thyself, a ground squirrel, it doesn't matter what — while you are thinking about being it?
        (2) And how can you not think about it when you see — inevitably, your eyes steal ahead — that the next item is "Think About It"?

2. Impersonality.
    a. You've got problems if you start using personal pronouns.
    b. Should it be
        (1) "Be Thyself," or
        (2) "Be Myself"?
            (a) If (1), then who is speaking?
            (b) If (2), then here I am, a grown man, saying "Be Myself" to myself. It's embarrassing.

III. Roman Numerals.
    A. Come to think of it, it is a good idea to start off with roman numerals. Otherwise, before you know it you are down to 1.a.(1)(a),

1. Which is scraping bottom,
2. Whereas I.A.1.*a.* leaves room for two more levels:
   a. I.A.1.*a.*(1).
   b. I.A.1.*a.*(1)(*a*).

B. On the other hand, no one has ever been able to follow a list of items headed by roman numerals.
   1. It goes back to the Ten Commandments.
   2. And as soon as you see *I*, even when it means "roman numeral one," you tend to think about yourself. The "I." And what a strange remove it is, that takes us to this notion of "the 'I.'" It is bad enough when someone named, say, Billy, goes around referring to himself as "Billy." If he should start talking about "the 'Billy'" — well, here we go down the rabbit hole. It's like those insurance companies now that will sell you a policy to cover (supposedly) your legal expenses in the event that you have to sue your insurance company for not paying off. Did you know that after a big high-rise luxury resort casino-hotel burns down and hundreds die, the hotel can insure itself *retroactively?* You or I couldn't, but a big outfit like that can. Somehow the hotel people and the insurance people all make out.

IV. Everything has to be parallel.

"Oh, you're getting way off into outlining," some may say. "Lists, kept in their place, are a servant to man." Uhm-hm. It is always a mistake to condescend to a list. You look at a list and say: "Well, now, this is a handy little prioritizational device. I should be able to knock all these items off bing bing bing." The list goes through a moment of quiet fusion and says: "Okay. Come on." Then try striking anything off it.

You never take the first item first, obviously. That would be like accepting the Russians' first offer in a disarmament talk: "Let me see if I have this straight. We transfer to you all of our military might except the generals and admirals, whom we get to keep, and you commit yourselves to an unspecified period of 'all due restraint.' Okay, what the hell."

But even the second item is not something you want to be drawn into precipitately. You look up and down the list and feel as though you are standing on one side of a stream, trying to decide which rock to put your foot on first. None of them look good.

I. It may very well be that a given item is not *right* for you when you come to it on a list.
II. It may very well be that in a free society, a given item is *by definition* not right for you when you come to it on a list.

Now it is time for lunch. As a rule, I have stopped drinking at lunch. It isn't fashionable to drink at lunch these days. But it used to be. I remember, years ago, when I first got a job in New York City. An old hand took me to lunch at a Chinese restaurant, treated himself to eight martinis, and fell — in stages, as if by peristalsis — all the way down a circular staircase that was ornamented to look like a dragon.

I. Some good nonalcoholic lunch beverages:
  A. Iced tea.
  B. Alka-Seltzer.
  C. Bireley's Chocolate Drink.
    1. If lunch is a peanut-butter log.
    2. And not many places today have peanut-butter logs.
    3. In fact, I don't remember the last time I saw:
      a. A peanut-butter log.
      b. A Bireley's Chocolate Drink.

II. Some bad nonalcoholic lunch beverages:
   A. Virgin margarita.
   B. Herbal old-fashioned.
   C. Bireley's Chocolate Drink.
      1. Now that I think about it.
      2. When I was a kid it was good, though:
         a. So was Nehi strawberry
         b. And Nugrape.
            (1) I don't think anything has ever struck me
                as prettier-colored than Nugrape foam
                back then.
            (2) Of course I was a child, and my tastes
                were unformed.
            (3) But in college English, when I came upon
                ". . . the blushful Hippocrene, / With
                beaded bubbles winking at the
                brim, / And purple-stainèd mouth," it
                brought Nugrape back.

Even when I don't drink, however, for a couple of hours
after lunch I feel listless. Before long it is nearly time to relax
and look back over the events of the day; and there haven't
been any yet.

I scan the list for a vulnerable spot. Sure, I could tack on
something easy, like "Memorize new apartment number."
But when you've seen as many digits come and go as I have,
what's so easy about that? Anyway, if I tacked it onto a list, I
wouldn't do it.

While I was not doing any of the things on my list for
today, I came across, in some of my papers, the following
list, "Gifts to Get for People," which dates back to December 1981.

1. *The Book of Lists* — Vaughn
2. *The Book of Lists II* — Beryl
3. *The Book of Sports Lists* — Artie

4. *The Book of Fish Lists* — Carl and Dot
5. *Listlust* — Hope
6. *Lost Lists of the Incas* — Oola
7. *The List Book Booklist* — Franz

I'll tell you something. That list did not give one iota.
Hey, Christmas is not a line-item affair. Christmas should
be cornucopious. Higgledy-piggledy down in the stocking
and under the tree. You wouldn't want to buy your turkey
by the inch, would you? You want partridges in pear trees
untold.

I remember when a cold-drink machine was a big, rusting,
red-metal box with a slide-open door in the top. You'd reach
down into that well of melting ice and variously shaped cold
bottles randomly heaped, and you'd swush around heavily
for a while and come up with a Nugrape. A Grapette. A Sun
Drop. An Orange Crush, with its pebbly, thick-walled bottle
the color of iodine. A Bireley's Chocolate Drink. Bireley's
put out an orange, too. A Nehi black cherry. Or it might be
something entirely new, that you'd never encountered before. Back then, TV marketing strategy was less advanced,
so if there was a new soft drink out, you might not have seen
a representation of it before you actually pulled one up out
of the ice and cold rivulets and ice flecks ran down it onto
your pulse and forearm.

Today a cold-drink machine is a list of buttons. Push one,
and a can comes down a chute.

Remember back even further — frankly, to the womb?
How your day developed? It was all very structured, very
symmetrical, but none of this by-the-numbers. You'd be reflecting, "Hmmmmn," and "I've got a heartbeat," and "I'm
not going to be a fish." But it wasn't:

1. "Hmmmmn."
2. "I've got a heartbeat."
3. "I'm not going to be a fish."

It was dawnings overlapping. You didn't know *what* you were going to be. Even if you had known, it wasn't anything you'd ever seen.

But you could sense the thread. And it wasn't linear. It was more like the thread on a screw, only preindustrial; something that turned to go forward. I'm holding out for a helical list. With a bubbling, grape-colored head.

BLUE YODEL 20

BARRY

I'm so tired of all this talk about "straight" and "gay." You cannot separate men into two camps, "straight" and "gay." That's just an effort to divide and weaken men. The truth is, there are two kinds of men: men who look good in a tank top and men who don't.

And the ones who do are insufferable.

My Cat Book Won't Come

"How's the big cat novel coming?" are the words I hate to hear. The average person cannot know how it feels to be under the gun as I have been — six and a half years struggling with the big one, the cat book to end them all. The longer it takes, the bigger it has to be. Every day, the question that I must live with grows: whether anything can be that big.

Get off of that!

Like a cat, I am out on a limb. And there is no calling the fire department. As I told Ted Koppel, on "Nightline," fire departments today don't get cats down out of trees. "What you are saying, if I may summarize, then, is this . . . ," said Koppel — those oddly catlike eyes never quite flicking.

"All I am saying," I snapped, "is that contemporary fire departments don't get cats down out of trees. 'You've never seen a cat skeleton in a tree, have you?' they ask." The skeletons of cat-book writers, on the other hand . . . The skeletons of true cat-book writers, I mean.

Get *off!*

To have declared openly, as I did on "The CBS Morning News," that the Garfield books are *not* cat books, because "Garfield is not only unamusing; Garfield does not convince as a cat," was to fling down a gauntlet before a consensus so entrenched, and so pleased with itself, that the issue is quite simply whose reputation will stand, mine or the literary establishment's. To have revealed in advance that my protagonist is a cat named Charles J. Guiteau was to take an enormous risk. To prove myself right about Garfield is to prove that millions of so-called cat-book lovers, and millions of professed *cat* lovers, are wrong in their love.

Get . . .

If one could extrapolate from fragments — as we do in our estimation of Sappho — the disinterested reader (but there are not even, appearances aside, any disinterested *cats*) would have to conclude that my book is, essentially, there. The chapter in which Guiteau's "owner," the chief justice of the U.S. Supreme Court, is racked by nightmares that he is Adolf Hitler — dreams accounted for, at length, when the justice wakes to find that Guiteau, for reasons of his own, has crept into the justice's bed and placed one paw beneath the justice's nose to create the sensation of a small black moustache — is done. And, according to those who have read it in manuscript, it is fine.

But do they know? Until *I* know, I cannot move on. And my confidante Irene calls it sexist to depict the chief justice of the U.S. Supreme Court as a man. Five times that chapter has undergone anguished recasting. Each time, I have felt that something of what should be its unexampled potency has eluded my slow, stretched, pawing reach.

Get off!

My friend Leo teaches deconstructive approaches to Latin American fiction, but you wouldn't know it to look at him out somewhere. I think he only does it because it's what's happening. He calls himself the Hillbilly Cat.

"Elvis was the Hillbilly Cat," I say.

"Was," he says.

"You're from White Plains, New York," I say.

"Gimme some slack," he says.

Last night he left Lon's Miracle Mile Lounge with a woman who was . . . tawny. All of a softness well toned. *I* had her scoped out. She looked pensive, enigmatic, I thought. I was waiting until after "Twilight Time," thinking it might seem prurient to ask a stranger to slow-dance first. Then the neo-fifties combo swung into "Sixty-Minute Man," and I was counting down, "Ten . . . nine . . . ," when Leo — before he can conceivably have known it was the right thing to do — went over to her table and took the painter's cap from her head (letting her hair flow down like butterscotch over a sundae) and put it on his own. He just now called to say she turned out to be a passionate attorney from Tulsa flushed with victory in a landmark harassment case, eager for a one-night romp punctuated by warm ablutions in her equally go-with-it friend Amber's condo pool, with flume, steam, shower-massage, and bubbler attachments.

If you don't get off of that . . . !

Guiteau is an "altered" cat. A modern cat, then. But how much of his character derives from that grim erotic neutrality, and how much from catness *an sich?* Can I ever know? Can I *feel* that I know? Guiteau's look is blank. The question burns.

Cats have no moral sense. Catch a dog on the couch and he leaps as if scalded and exclaims: "I'm off! I'm off the couch now! Oh, Lord! I wasn't ... I was just ... I was guarding it! *Dogs can sense when someone is about to break in and steal a couch and* ... Oh! I can't lie to you! To *you*, after all you've done for me! I was on the couch! How could I ... I *know* better. You *know* I know better. I just ..."

Catch a cat on the couch and it doesn't even shrug.

Dialogue does not flow from a cat. A cat does not even know its name. Or care. A cat has unreadable eyes.

Yet the books pour out. *Keeping Tabs* remained on the *New York Times* best-seller list for ninety-one consecutive weeks. In acquiring the film rights to *Another Man's Persian*, Avram Zorich went to eight figures. *Real Cats Don't Eat Couscous*, for all its dragged-in anti-Islamism, captivated reviewers from coast to coast. Marisha N. Puhl's *Kitten Kin*, with its sepia-tone photos of pipe-smoking, etc., kittens as archetypal "Uncle Ned," etc., struck me as too cute. Her *Kits, Cats, Sex and Wives* I found, frankly, lurid. Yet Puhl's sales, hardback and paper combined, have passed the four million mark. I happen to know that Amsler Rizell, author of *Life with a Purrpuss*, bought his first cat — *by mail* — in order to get a book out of it.

Get *off* of that!

The only writer in the field today who commands my respect is the French critic Yves Sevy-Ouiounon, who raises such questions as (my translation) "What must the cats look like who enter — as they must, else art is fraud — the world of Mickey Mouse?" Sevy-Ouiounon's thought breaks frames.

As do cats. The soft touch (with the poufy foot that seems never to *weigh* upon anything), the cherished photo toppled from the desk ... I have paid my dues. Cats have intercepted my footsteps at the ankle for so long that my gait, both at home and on tour, has been compared to that of a man wading through low surf. And in my book it shows.

Get off!

Only someone whose domestic atmosphere has been permeated with cat hair for more than three decades could have conceived the plot-point whereby my assassin is unmasked. The mailer of the threatening note is a cat owner (cats themselves, *pace* Garfield, cannot use the postal service) who is too frugal to throw away the first two inches every time he uses Scotch tape, and who has neglected to fit his tape dispenser with a screen covering the exposed lower surface of that first strip of tape between roll and cutter, so that when he uses tape to affix the letters scissored from magazines to the sheet of paper from which the watermark has been removed, he uses — on the first two letters — tape to which adhere traceable cat hairs.

Get off of that.

I would not wish to leave the impression that my cat book is a thriller merely. That I have felt compelled to plot it so strongly — nine deaths — reflects the cultural conservatism (of which cats are part and parcel: dogs are Democrats; cats, Republicans) pervading the arts today. The book's indwelling ambition far transcends "story." What the book would do would be as near unknowable as the animal entailed. *Intrinsically*, the book would pounce, loll, and go *m'rowr*; would present thee with felinity for a while.

Some mused-upon titles, none right:

> *Cat's Up!*
> *More Ways Than One*
> *Unkindest Cat*
> *Tabby La Raza*
> *Now I'm the King*

To enter the world of my cat book is to enter an ancient consciousness, an abysmal shallows, in whose context narrative focus, as the contemporary book-buyer knows it, is as *arriviste* a notion as foot reflexology. (Which Leo has taken up. Purely to meet women.) It will not be an easy book to read. It is not easy in the writing. There have been repeated setbacks involving my own cat and the physical manuscript. Get off of that. I'm telling you, Mieu-Mieu, *get off of that.* I swear, *I'll wring your neck!* I mean it! *Mieu . . .*

A dog book comes when summoned. A cat book, when it will.

BLUE YODEL 21

CLAUDE

Why do female dogs mount other dogs, of both sexes, and people's legs? This is a question that has troubled male thinkers, strictly among themselves, for centuries. Not a word of this immemorial discussion has been recorded in writing, although Henry Kissinger almost let a reference to it slip in 1972, in the famous interview with Oriana Fallaci (in which he did reveal that he saw himself as a cowboy). Whenever men get together without women, the question arises.

For one thing, it throws the whole concept of "doing it dog-style" into ambiguity. For another thing, the female dogs don't seem to do it to be fashionable, or for spite, or to get out of housework. They seem to have an instinct to get up on top from behind and hump.

For some reason, feminists have never picked up on this. Someday they are bound to — in support of what skewed assertion, God only knows. Men keep trying to have an explanation ready.

So far, it is believed, the best explanation is one that Kissinger hit upon one evening, in conversation with John Kenneth Galbraith.

"*Female cats do not do this! Correct?*"

"*I have never seen one.*"

"*So it is not sexual at all! Female dogs do it to prove they are not cats!*"

Whether this explanation will do, when the crunch comes, is not at all clear to most men. So the question remains; just one more of those things that men have to worry about, and women don't.

Secrets of the Apple

TELLING the Apple what my first name was. That was my mistake. I have been married only twice, both times to women who called me by my first name. When a machine says to me something like **GOOD, ROY! YOU FOUND IT QUICKLY!** (**IT** being the return key), I feel patronized. But also . . . engaged.

For the purpose of this essay, an Apple II was placed in my home for a week. I thought, well sure. I had always wanted to give a computer a piece of my mind.

But I was put on the defensive as soon as I opened the big box the Apple was delivered in. I found some smaller boxes and a sheet of instructions, which advised me to be careful in opening the smaller boxes: "Those staples bite!"

Now, I have been bitten by staples many a time. But that is my lookout. If this carton of not-even-assembled-yet stuff had decided *after getting to know me better* that I deserved to be addressed as if I were its kindergarten pupil, well, all right, maybe.

As it happened, I had already been bitten, by the staples in that first big box. When Eve got into the apple, I suppose it said, "Those snakes lie." Great, now you tell me. "Those staples bite!" indeed! Also, that was the only part of the instructions I could understand. I withdrew from the carton with dignity.

Within twenty-four hours my daughter Ennis had assembled the Apple II in her bedroom, had hooked it up to her portable TV, and had figured out how to destroy the entire advancing horde of hideous aliens in the Stellar Invaders game without being wiped out herself. And my son John had given the Apple Adventure game a ribald instruction. The machine's response, which offended both children's sense of delicacy, was **YOUR PLACE OR MINE?**

That same question, preceded by **IS THIS**, was one I might well have addressed to the Apple. The Apple loomed large in my home. It had got my children to talking in terms of dwarves, RF Modulators, cursors, and diskettes. Its beeps were more pervasive than the sounds of the heating system. Friends and neighbors would come to our door, walk right past me, and go upstairs to visit the computer.

It was time for me to take the Apple in hand. I went upstairs and yelled at it. It didn't respond. Then, somehow, there crept into my consciousness a little electronic-sounding wheedle: **WHATEVER YOU DO, PLEASE DON'T THROW ME INTO THE BRIAR PATCH. THAT IS, PLEASE DON'T INSERT THE DISKETTE LABELED "APPLE PRESENTS . . . APPLE" INTO MY DISK DRIVE AND START LEARNING HOW TO GIVE ME COMMANDS.**

So I did. And it wasn't long before the machine had discovered my first name, and was using it to give *me* commands. And when I had proved to the Apple my ability to type out **YES,** or something along those lines, it would ask me, **ISN'T THAT NEAT?**

I refused to answer such a question. But the Apple didn't acknowledge my refusal. And when I tried to get down to brass tacks by asking, **IF APPLE > THE BLOUNTS THEN PROVE IT** it responded by saying, **SYNTAX ERROR.**

That got my back up. Syntax is my bread and butter. As I say, however, I felt . . . engaged. I gritted my teeth and inserted the Apple Writer–system diskette. I chose that diskette because I had always been afraid that some day a distinguished periodical would call me up and say: "We'd like to send you out to cover Armageddon on a fat expense account. Of course you'll have to file your copy on an Electronic Word Gizmo."

After a couple of hours with the Apple Writer, I felt prepared for such an assignment. I was even able to delete not-quite-trenchant phrases from my copy and then, if I felt nostalgic for them, to retrieve them from the automatic "storage buffer."

"Nice little gizmo here," I found myself thinking.

But then the Apple's storage buffer gave me a serious turn. I was composing merrily, humming the old Apple right along, pretending I was covering the 1984 Big Brother Nominating Convention. I hit the retrieval key by mistake, and the following word marched resolutely into my text: **BLAGNONY.**

I hadn't stored any **BLAGNONY** *in the buffer.* I didn't even know what it meant. But it looked insulting. This machine was not content to snipe at my syntax. It was now slinging an obscure, Hungarian-sounding epithet at, *and into,* my reportage.

But I'll tell you what I did. I didn't explode. I sat there for a few minutes and used the old bean. And this is what I realized: **BLAGNONY** was the sum of a series of individual typos that I had deleted and that the buffer had mindlessly (to my way of thinking) stored.

"You know what, Apple?" I crowed (orally). "You aren't telling me anything! You are a lower form of life than I am! You just sit there, like a clam, responding to stimuli!

And even a clam would know better than **B** . . . **L** . . . **A** . . .
G . . . **N** . . . **O** . . **N** . . . **Y** in, **BLAGNONY** out!"

I went back through the "Apple Presents . . . Apple" program. And this time I lied. I told the Apple my name was
Norton. The Apple would tell me things like **YOU'RE
MAKING GREAT PROGRESS, NORTON!** "And you're
a neat little machine, Kumquat," I would chuckle (orally). I
felt retrieved.

BLUE YODEL 22

WES

*All I know is, living with a woman's love is like swimming
with a fish in your arms. You're astonished how you glide.
But let your attention dry and the fish will flinch and go
deep, and you feel it leave, and you know you didn't hold it
right, and once you begin to feel it move away it's gone.*

*You probably never were holding it right. It may never
have known it was in your arms. How can you have consid-
ered the fish so cuddly, and how can the fish have felt that
you were so marine?*

*Don't coast. Take on water. Some people are really rotten
toward the fish — toward the fish — and it stays.*

*Don't tell the fish that you can't breathe underwater.
Don't break the water down into H's and O's.*

How to Sportswrite Good

I READ with pleasure nearly every form of sportswriting, from Tug McGraw's "Scroogie" comic strip to "Ebony Fisherman," a black angling column in *The New Pittsburgh Courier*. "Scroogie" once showed a manager sitting in his dugout reflecting: "I can't believe it! It's too good to be true!! All I do is sit on my hands for nine innings and we *plaster* Pittsburgh nine-one!!! [Pause] Just think what we could do if I sat on my *fists!!*"

I scour *The Sporting News* for great passages, like this one from a story about an Oriole batboy who had hooks instead of fingers: "He is going to major in mathematics. I could have told him that it's hard to become good in mathematics when you don't have any fingers to count on, and I'm sure he would have gotten a sincere laugh out of it." Sportswriting is like country music: it is sometimes very good, and sometimes when it is really bad it is even better. And it can be largely silly and genuinely worth something at the same time.

But I don't want to read any *tomes* about sports. That is what two books — *Sports in America*, by James Michener, and *The Joy of Sports*, by Michael Novak — look like to me: tomes. Well, I would read a tome about some particular *aspect* of sports — *The Dribble in America* or *The Joy of Batting Orders*. I would cherish a nice snappy treatment that knocked sports, in essence, right into the creek, as old SCLC campaigner Hosea Williams did incidentally on a BBC TV special, when he criticized the city of Atlanta for allotting tax money to a golf course: "*Damn* some grass to knock a ball on when there are people in the streets robbing for food."

But I don't want to read anything in which somebody steps back and takes a long view of *Sport as Something It Is High Time We Faced Up to the Big Picture and Tiny Epiphanies of; or, Why We Like to Watch People Spring Through the Air and Land in a Heap.* Hasn't everybody always down through the ages liked to watch people spring through the air and land in a heap? I'd rather read *The Wit and Wisdom of Herman Hickman* or *Among the Brownies: The Ordeal of Ned Garver.*

A while back, there was even a flurry of writing — in *Esquire, More,* the *Los Angeles Times* and probably *Playgirl* and *Presbyterian Life* — about sportswriting. Writing about sportswriting seemed an odd exercise, like going worm fishing to catch worms, but I enjoyed reading it when it didn't get too abstract. Sportswriters have interesting day-to-day problems. Consider Ted Colton, then of the *McKeesport* (Pennsylvania) *Daily News,* being chased through the Three Rivers Stadium parking lot by a whole irate Steeler fan club, led by a man in a gorilla suit, for picking Cleveland to take the AFC Central. Or Pete Axthelm of *Newsweek,* stepping glumly into the Pittsburgh locker room after the 1979 Super Bowl, surveying the jubilance, and saying, "I can't stand to look at a team that hasn't beaten the spread and thinks it's *won.*"

I don't guess anyone is going to make a movie about an intrepid pair of sportswriters. In sports novels sportswriters are always wimps or drunks or sneaks or hacks, or all four. In life they are often abject straight men. A writer asked Alex Johnson, then with the Cincinnati Reds, "Alex, you hit only two homers all last year, and this season you already have seven. What's the difference?" And Alex answered, "Five." Once Bill Bradley's sole response to a reporter who asked him why the Knicks had fined him one hundred dollars was, "You have a stupid job."

But when Henry Aaron dumped strawberries on Frank Hyland of the *Atlanta Journal* for something Hyland wrote,

Hyland got letters of support "from every red-neck in the country. One even wanted me to run for president," Hyland told me one spring training, when I found myself talking with, at the same time, him and Pat Livingston of the *Pittsburgh Press*, whom Mean Joe Greene once spat on. For his part, Livingston said that a guy in a Pittsburgh bar who was dying of cancer anyway offered to shoot Greene for him, but Livingston said no.

I am trying to conceive of a big movie action scene in which sportswriters would be central. I mean one where the sportswriters wouldn't have spit or strawberries all over them. Sportswriters can be good vigorous drinking arguers. "Stop calling me an asshole!" I remember one scribe yelling to another at the height of a group debate during dinner (paid for by the team we were covering) in a fancy San Francisco restaurant. "I'm on *your side* and you're calling me an asshole!"

In *The Joy of Sports*, Michael Novak proposes that "newspaper and magazine writers, regaining their faith in words, should describe the contests on the field as if no one watched television. . . . The human spirit needs words, needs the irony, the subtlety, and the bite of words, and above all the capacity of words to go beneath surfaces, their power to pull aside veils and uncover unsuspected dimensions of human striving. Many regions of athletic experience have scarcely been explored."

Right. But I wonder whether Novak has any real sense of the linguistic problems sportswriters are up against. When athletes speak most naturally about what they do, they tend to use graphic, anatomical language. "I'm gonna be right up in his noseholes," said Joe Frazier. "That pitch I threw, the muscle stay back, the bone keep going," Luis Tiant said, explaining how something snapped in his arm. Athletes can even slap a quick metaphor on you. The Redskins' Larry Brown, asked which runners he had modeled himself on, said: "I've watched Kelly. He was an out-of-sight runner. I can't have the moves that Kelly has. I can't create the moves that Sayers made. I have my own style. I want to be my own man. When I was a kid I used to watch Jimmy Brown and all I can say is if you got a loaded gun, you fire it."

Now you might say that such quotes are a boon to the sportswriter. (And don't you think Norman Mailer would have loved saying what Brown said, substituting Hemingway for Jimmy Brown?) The only trouble is this: How are you going to write vividly enough *in between* the good quotes to keep your column from looking like a couple of pearls set in a hunk of pot metal?

More often, the problem with players' language is that, in Gertrude Stein's phrase, it is "inaccrochable." *Sports Illustrated* prints a great deal of lively athletic language. Its "They Said It" column is the best running collection of quotes in any publication of any kind that I know of. But it is also a family magazine, which once changed the word *crap* in a story of mine to *baloney*. In a family magazine you can't print what *SI*'s Ron Fimrite says he once heard a ballplayer in batting practice exclaim: "I couldn't hit my motherfucking grandmother!"

Sometimes players' language is not only unquotable but sort of otherworldly. Players can make a football game, for instance, sound like a struggle between two grand corporate rumps and their crewmen:

> When it come down to it, we flat got our ass in gear and moved the ball on their ass. Chops was yelling at 'em in the line, "Just keep on throwing all that quick-popping shit at our ass — we're gonna *bury* your ass." Once we got our ass jacked up and started coming, it was their *ass*. We hit our ass off out there, didn't we?

But players' language is standard English compared to coaches'. One afternoon in the University of Tennessee football press box I realized that I could hear every word that a UT coach, in the next booth over, was saying to his colleagues on the field via a headphone hookup. Here is roughly how the fourth quarter went:

He can't bite down too hard on the tight end till he finds out what Z is doing. You see what I mean?

Okay now break on three watch the screen. You got tango? Watch the screen, watch the screen.

SCREEN! All right. Holler down there and tell Carmichael. . . . Aw, we missed three.

Seven-five holes! Seven-five holes!

Tango, tango, c'mon Ed, watch the slip screen. Slip screen . . . power.

Tell the corners to funnel and flow away, and watch the Y. And you watch Z, now.

Off. All right, they in man again.

Watch the option, watch the option. Sprint draw! Sprint draw! Watch out now, watch out, *God dang it.* Oh no! Great play.

Tell that backside end to crank up. Tell them backers to crank it now! Crank it!

Watta ya got? *Bluff* the side coverage, Mo. *Bluff* the side coverage, Mo.

Tell that Watts to get in there on that guy! *God* dog. *Ahrrghlk.*

Pow'r one! Pow'r one! Gonna be the Pitt sweep. Gonna be the Pitt sweep. Guaran*tee* you!

Nope.

You got to really come out there and collision that tight end coming down there. . . . Number two, tell Jerry four coverage, get them people cranked up.

Let's go defense. Forty-four tango! All right, what they got? Forty-four tango?

All right, let's go. Power.

Watch the pass, now, watch the pass. Holler at 'em, "Pass!" Pass! Holler, "*Pass!!*"

Either pass or Pitt sweep . . . pow'r. . . .

Let's go, offense. Stick it in 'em! Give 'em hell! Aw.

Let's go, defense. Loosen off. Loosen off. Tell the tango end to loosen off some. Loosen off the tango end! Loosen off, Art! Tell Poole to get the curl!

Oskie.

Tell Wheeler to walk off a little bit, as the tango end.

All right! [Great rumble arises, partition shakes.] Give 'em hell!

Aw. Well, hell, I don't care — we got the damn ball I don't care if they put it back to the damn four, now. Give 'em hell, Carruthers. Woooooeee.

So there it was. I had the whole inside story. But what was my lead going to say? "Outlined against a grey November sky, the Vols edged the Commodores yesterday as Mo bluffed the side coverage, the tango loosened off, and the corners funneled and flowed away"?

Oh, I could go on and on about the word problems of a sportswriter. For instance, when players adopt coaches' language, you get remarks like "That revenge factor is sweet" (Glenn Doughty, Baltimore Colts) and "Then that injury factor happened" (Norm Snead, passim). It is little wonder that sportswriters tend to lose perspective themselves and blurt out expressions like "doffed his erstwhile nonentity" to mean "became famous."

But maybe coaches are right, and it is best to look at problems positively, to regard them as opportunities. Sometimes I look at a piece of sportswriting and think . . .

Well, one afternoon I looked at these two paragraphs:

"I know I've got two games tomorrow and milestones aren't going to be much help," Willie Stargell of the Pittsburgh Pirates said.

"When you're playing you just have to grind it out," he added.

And I thought, "You can't grind it out with milestones," and for a moment a whole world opened up, of worn-out sports imagery recast: a graduating receiver hauling in the sheepskin, down linemen made of duck feathers, a New York Knick condemned by a witch doctor's curse to a lifetime of moving *within* the ball . . .

Well, I don't know. But the sports pages and the comic sections are the only places in a newspaper where you can still fool around verbally. Maybe someone will take advantage of this freedom and transform sportswriting into a wild macaronic poetry, in which different frames of mind entangle across metaphysical lines of scrimmage. On the other hand, maybe sports headline writers will straighten up just a bit and stop writing headlines like LEUKEMIA THROWS DUSTER AT TWINS' THOMPSON.

People shouldn't sell sportswriters short, anyway. "Regaining their faith in words," indeed! We do have a certain pride, a sense of calling. There is the story about a scribe who showed up in the press box after a game too drunk to write even if he had seen anything that had happened. Firmly within the tradition of old-time sportswriting, he appealed to another scribe to let him copy the story he had just filed.

"Well, I don't know," the sober scribe said.

"Come on," pleaded the drunk scribe.

"But I hate to . . ."

"Come on, please."

The sober scribe said oh, okay, and handed over a carbon of his story. The drunk scribe cranked paper into his typewriter and started copying. He got through three paragraphs before he stopped and looked off into the distance.

"To think," he sighed, "that I would be reduced . . . to copying shit like this."

BLUE YODEL 23

MARTIN

I head up ARMA, the American Real Male Association, a nonprofit corporation dedicated to the countering of feminist disinformation.

There is a certain virulent women's faction that is trying to put over the notion that men who argue at length about whether Enos "Country" Slaughter scored from first on a single in the 1942 or, rather, the 1946 World Series are making it all up, in an effort to make women feel that there is a vast area of human history that they will never know about. (Which is true, they won't.)

Enos "Country" Slaughter, these women will tell you, is mythical, and so are, for instance, what they describe as "the 'Brooklyn' Dodgers." The first actual major-league baseball game, they contend, was played in 1958, when a group of women promoters, having stumbled upon the secret that baseball was all "an interior game" in men's minds, decided to make a killing, and staged a game between Milwaukee and Los Angeles — which had not yet even been in the allegedly mythical major leagues. These women then had to be bought off by a hastily assembled committee of men, one of whom was designated Enos "Country" Slaughter and was assigned, for reasons of high visibility, to the New York Yankees, for whom he batted .204. Baseball has not been the same since, but men are in no position to complain. (Some of these same women — according to this bra-burning bilge — went on to found the aerospace industry, which, admittedly, took most of the fun out of rocket ships.)

Now anyone who knows baseball history can see immediately how clumsily cobbled together this crackpot theory is.

For instance, Enos "Country" Slaughter hit .304 in 1958. But there are millions of people in the world who do not know baseball history, and these include women in the computer industry, for instance, who could take over control of baseball statistics tomorrow. If you open up the Baseball Encyclopedia *some day and it says "Slaughter, Enos Bradsher 'Country' (real name Rene Pinkle), 1958–59, lifetime B.A. .169" or some such god damn piece of outright god damn fiction, you'll know that the grisly specter of these women has prevailed.*

God damn it, Country Slaughter came up with the Cards in the late Gashouse Gang era and played nineteen years on guts and hustle and his lifetime batting average was .300! Exactly! And that is true and that will always be true whatever vicious plot may strike at the vitals of what we know to be true.

I saw the son of a bitch play in the 1942 World Series! The one when he scored from first — actually it was on an infield out!

Anyway my father did.

But try to tell women that!

The Truth about History

I guess you saw the headlines: SO YOU SWALLOWED GEORGE'S WOODEN TEETH? GET THEM OUT OF YOUR HEAD — DENTAL HISTORIAN. There is no way, historians now agree, that George Washington could have had wooden teeth.

Okay? First the cherry tree, now the teeth. Another old chestnut tossed onto the fire by the spoilsport, or "No, Virginia," school of historiography.

The trouble with historians, they don't like a good story. Or a good line. "You know what Sherman said . . . ," you begin to say, and they interrupt: Sherman didn't really say "War is hell." Actually he said either "Well, well" or "Well, hell"; there is no telling what he had on his mind. And Babe Ruth didn't really call his shot in the 1932 World Series. He was actually signaling to a vendor in the bleachers for a frank. Several years ago, I remember, a couple of French historians declared that there was no Joan of Arc. Never was one. Best just forget her.

We all know what prompts these disclosures. Some historian starts telling his class about Joan of Arc. "This morning we take up the story of a simple shepherd girl who . . ."

"Oh, no," the class groans. (Because they are all jaded sophomores.) "Not that again."

"Well, not a word of it is true," the historian says, hastily; and then he begins to improvise.

It is easy to tear things down, History! What are you going to give us to take their place? If Joan of Arc wasn't a simple shepherd girl who had visions and led the French against the English at Orléans and went on to be burned at the stake and played by Ingrid Bergman and Jean Seberg, then who was?

No one, according to these French historians. The whole thing was a publicity stunt. Joan was actually a girl of royal blood who was brought out at Orléans for morale purposes. She wasn't executed at all. She later married someone named Robert.

What a charming tale. What are we supposed to do now, when Joan of Arc's birthday comes around? Reflect on what a kick it must have given Joan and Robert (pronounced "Ro-bair") in their declining years to sit at home and chuckle about all the crazy legends a girl can start if she will play along with the military?

When that story came out, it didn't just spoil Joan of Arc for me. It spoiled history as a whole. I threw up my hands. I became willing to accept that nothing ever happened in ages past that couldn't be reduced to simple administrative terms, or worse.

Rasputin was just a minor Russian official who had a little something going with the tsarina, and she worked up a disguise for him that everyone but the tsar saw through from the beginning. He died in a boating accident.

Mohandas Gandhi was actually a portly behind-the-scenes type who dressed, mutatis mutandis, like Colonel Tom Parker, except that — in the curious belief that it would impress the English — he carried a shillelagh. For photo opportunities, of course, there were the several interchangeable, wizened stand-ins.

Cleopatra was a man, and not even a very prepossessing one, who, as a matter of fact, was immune, because of the quantities of garlic he ate, to asp venom.

The historical Charlemagne wasn't a man but rather a primitive committee.

Vincent van Gogh never set foot outside the town of Bort-les-Orgues, France, and his mother painted all of his best things. The famous mailed decapitated ear was a figment of the public-relations firm engaged by van Gogh's dealer — himself not an imaginative person. Actually, van Gogh never had a mistress, and took both of his ears to the grave. Indeed, the only reason that the outsized woolen cap his mother made him wear never slipped completely down over his eyes was that his ears were always so large and firmly attached. He never had any moods, incidentally, to speak of.

Romulus and Remus were no more suckled by a wolf than you and I and Henry Steele Commager were. They were suckered on a wharf.

Then I snapped back out of italics and started to think: "History, wait a minute. You owe me more than that." I can understand why historians resist being doomed to repeat themselves, but why don't they try making historical figures *more* numinous, instead of less? That's what the average person would do, if he or she had the chance to be a historian.

Millard Fillmore. If the truth be told, Fillmore would roll into the Oval Office about 9:45 in the morning after being up half the night playing Whigs and Masons with Henry Clay. Whigs and Masons was a wrestling game. It is said — even if not by historians — that Fillmore would summon Alex H. H. Stuart, his secretary of the interior, to tie his (Fillmore's) right foot to his (again, Fillmore's) left arm and then he (yes, Fillmore) would still throw Clay four times in five.[1] Of Whigs and Masons, Fillmore was the Magic Johnson.

But after getting into the office a couple of hours behind everybody else — and you know the secretaries are all grumbling because why should they be at their desks hitting it bright and early when the president was out till all hours horsing around — Fillmore would immediately put everyone in a dynamic, progressive frame of mind by telling how he bested legendary riverman Mike Fink in a gator-cowing contest. (Fillmore, in only a breechclout, once cowed a twelve-hundred-pound gator just by going "Well?" at it. This has been *documented*.)

Then Fillmore would make a statement of national purpose so clearly put and deeply felt that all those who heard him, however small their roles in the government's workings, felt lifted and involved. "This," Fillmore's listeners felt, "is why we must hold our great plural union together,

1. Ironically enough quite an extrovert, Stuart was a real pistol in his own right whose mother, a seeress, had imparted unto him the power literally to contain multitudes. It is from his middle initials alone that we derive not only Hubert Humphrey and Herbert Hoover but also Horace Heidt.

and never let it succumb to meanness or fixed ideas. And here," the White House staff and any average citizens on hand would reflect, "is one who is larger than we, yet one of us."

At which juncture Clay might pop in, tousled from the night before. (No matter what *he* had been up to, Fillmore always arrived for business looking cleaner than the Board of Health.) Fillmore would wink at Clay's stout, scuffed Kentucky brogans and lighten the moment with a remark about "feet of Clay," which Clay himself — being possessed of a firm yet unoppressive sense of his own authenticity — would take in good spirits.

Another thing about Fillmore. He never secretly taped his telephone conversations.

BLUE YODEL 24

ARNOLD

Ever ask women why their shirts button backwards? Blouses. They don't know. They don't know their own heritage.

If you push them, they may say something about lobes of the brain. It has nothing to do with lobes of the brain. And don't believe the various myths you hear: When Adam and Eve were expelled from the Garden, Jehovah saith, "HENCEFORTH tHOU SHALT KNOW tHY NAKEDNESS AND WEAR RAIMENT, A SHIRT ALONE COULD RUN yOU THIRTY, FORTY SHEKELS. AND yOU" — turning to Eve — "GOT TO BUTTON yOURS BACKWARDS." No. They didn't even have buttons then.

It's not so men and women won't get confused unbuttoning each other, either. Or so they will be confused. I've heard it both ways.

The blouse was invented by Louis Blouse (1678–1734) of France. A woman was shirty to him one day in the street and he said, "Tiens. Voyons-nous à propos cette attitude-là," and went home and developed the blouse. This was in 1716. It buttoned backwards.

And all it does, it just makes women wonder and repress. Repressed wondering is a strong thing. You ever, when you were a little kid, suddenly notice — say your name was Mel Lemton, suddenly it comes to you when you've learned to print your name that Lemton is not Mel backwards? Maybe somebody's telling you something! And you repress it for ten or twelve years, or more. Meanwhile, you're probably dyslexic. And it's eating on you deep down inside that you're not who you are.

That's how blouses affect women. Along those lines. Blouse did it on purpose. And so you read in Virginia Woolf's diaries, at the end of a particularly trying day for her: "Why is it that our blouses button backward, again? Oh well."

(An attempt was made to canonize Blouse in 1923, but the American church objected that there was already a St. Louis Blues.)

Why Not
Active People *in* Beer?

HERE'S what I'm hearing. Television is saturated with sports. And televised sports is saturated with commercials. So, where's growth?

Let's get down to basics. What supports sports? Television. What supports television? Advertising. But what runs sports? Television. What kind of deal is this? Advertising runs television, sure. But it lets television run sports. What does television let advertising have? The *time-outs!*

And, okay, a few other things. Tennis on TV, the players got logos on their shoes, socks, shorts, shirt, wristbands, headband, and racket strings.

But let me ask you something. Does a tennis player have legs? Hell yes, a tennis player has legs. Do women look at tennis players' legs? Are women a market? Can legs be tattooed?

Then there's the *court!* It's a wasteland! How long has tennis been on TV now? Quarter of a century? And nobody's put ads on the court? It's like Alaska with nobody digging in it.

Hockey. All that ice. Why no blowup of a beer can with beads of moisture? Yeah, it would show through. If not, we replace the ice with a polymer that doesn't scratch but looks like ice. Looks more like ice than the real thing. You think a nice blown-up cool one wouldn't look good under there?

Or, you know what *E.T.* did for Reese's Pieces. Well, what if each base in baseball is the likeness of an M&M? Or, you want to stick with traditional colors, a Cert.

Back to tennis. Serve ticks the net, right? Some pale sweaty guy in a suit and tie with his nose on the tape says, "Let."

"Let," and that's all. And the announcer's got to think of something to add. "Boy, Lendl sure is hitting a lot of lets this set." What good does that do *anybody?* Twenty million people sitting there wondering what product to buy next, and they're hearing, "Boy, Lendl is sure . . ."

"Let." Think a minute. What's a natural here? The net judge takes a hike for all time and we replace him with a little technology. A little technology that, when the serve ticks the net, we hear, "Let . . .'s have another cup of coffee, let's have a cup of Nescafé." And maybe there's a few bucks in it for the announcers if they start saying, "Boy, Lendl sure has hit a lot of Nescafés this set." You can't *buy* advertising like that. Not unless we get cracking.

What is going to save this nation's economy? This tennis guy Yannick Noah gets a little more arc? No. More people *buying* things, is what. How do you get people to buy things? *Remind* them.

Swimming. Nobody's done *anything* with swimming. You know why? Hidebound thinking. Let me ask you a question. Swimming *has* to be in water? Who *says*? People have just blindly *assumed* it has to be in water. Swimming can't be in 7-Up?

Bound to produce faster times. Hey, times get faster anyway, don't they? Why shouldn't somebody's product get credit? So, an enhanced public awareness of the energy you get from 7-Up. *Or* Canada Dry, *or* Perrier, *or* — hey, a nice visual — Champale. Beer's *pretty*, right? (Who proved that? Advertising.) Active people *with* beer are pretty, right? Why not active people *in* beer?

How much you think it would be worth to beverage companies — this is spillover, here, beyond TV — if sportswriters get in the habit of writing, "Tracy Caulkins cleft the Gatorade for a new world record over 100 yellow-green yards today and emerged feeling 'more refreshed but less relaxed' than she felt last month after winning the NCAA finals in a pool of Almadén Lite."

Nicknames. Nicknames is a whole area. They called Brooks Robinson "Hoover," right? Because he sucked up grounders. Let me ask you, did any ad agency get a piece of that? Get a little *splinter* of that? No. Does it have to be that way? The way I see it, it only has to be that way if we stand by and *let* it be that way.

A Nickname Board. There are guys in sports with a talent for attracting nicknames. There are guys in sports with a talent for giving nicknames. Get these guys together. With our guys. Work out a deal.

It's too late now for Larry "Sanka" Csonka or Stan "The Manufacturer's Hanover" Musial, but how about Jim "Minute" Rice. Dennis and John "Johnson & Johnson" Johnson. Moses "AT&T" (for "Awful Tough and Tall") Malone.

Liquor, we know, can't be advertised on TV. But what if Mark Fidrych comes back as not just The Bird but The Wild Turkey? Isn't it his right?

Doctors, we know, can't advertise. But would it be advertising exactly if, say, a certain great basketball star, say, could find it worth his while to become known as Julius "Dr. J. L. Holtz, DDS, 12 Park Avenue" Erving?

Then there's *events*. The Disneyworld Series. National Soup Council might talk it over with Pete Rozelle, the possibility of making it the Souper Bowl every January. It's a thought. It's something to kick around. Listen, Pete Rozelle is not deaf to a little ancillary.

Understand, I'm not saying slip a little consideration directly to the commissioner. Come on, these people, these are not the kind of people you approach that way. The level of individual you are dealing with in sports today, they do things on principle. And that principle is one that the advertising industry shares wholeheartedly: maximizing profitability.

Okay, awards. In baseball we've already got the Rolaids Award for relief pitchers. How about if the National Greengrocers Association recognizes, each season, for the highest batting average on natural turf, a Most Vegetable Player. For the most knockdowns by an Afro-American boxer every year, there's the Black & Decker trophy.

But that's official stuff. What we need to cut into is word of mouth. See, this thing, in its importance, transcends sports. It transcends *television*, almost. Tell me if I'm wrong: the advertising industry, for years, forever, has been trying to get a piece of word of mouth. Right? This thing is the breakthrough.

Remember Watergate? Did Watergate boost the Mexican-food industry? *Had* to. *Had* to. All that talk about the Big Enchilada. And *free. Zip* it cost the boys over at Frijole Roller Inc. Not centavo uno. That, friends, is *wrong.*

So. Get the various games' phrasemakers together. Couldn't the new word for a bases-loaded homer be a "Mr. Clean"? Couldn't it be "Top Job" instead of "topspin lob"?

Okay. But just one thing. I want to say this to you, a serious word. It goes without saying, we would never do anything, never introduce any new thinking, no matter how beautiful, that would affect the integrity of the game. Any game. In fact, I see a public-service message from the National Ad Council:

"Sports. Advertising. The Great American Games. Hand in hand through the years, respecting each other's space. Picture your ads in it."

The integrity of the *language.* And of the *visuals.* That's what we're after.

BLUE YODEL 25

COOPER

Of course you can't tell women about infidelities. Why would you?

The thing is, you can't tell them about fidelities. There are a lot of guys who are faithful. And sometimes they want to tell her, "I'm faithful to you!" It is boiling up in their heart, they want to testify.

But don't testify. You can't testify. For one thing, say you testify to your fidelity and then one night you brush against a Paraguayan woman with honey-colored skin at the Fluid Dynamics / Coupled Fluid Dynamics and Chemical Kinetic

Phenomena Conference you are attending in Tampa and she leans forward — surprising herself, too, actually — so as to brush against you again. . . . One night, and the woman to whom you are faithful one hundred percent except for this one highly specialized case — one night — and she finds out about it. And that means you've been lying the whole time before. Which is maybe fourteen years. Right?

But even if there never was a Paraguayan! They don't believe you! You say, fidelity, and they say, "That's nice," and won't listen. They don't believe you! You know why men lie to women so much? Because women don't believe them anyway! Or they believe them in this sort of separate sphere. There's this separate sphere that they keep everything you say in. And they believe you, on this sort of nonfactual basis. I think women always regard men on this nonfactual basis. By "factual" I mean what you think of as factual. Sincerely think of.

You are this specialized character in this strange drama they have in their heads.

Did you ever see a play by a woman? Didn't you think it was on some kind of strange kind of, I don't know . . . level? It wasn't! Not to them! That's straight to them! They have this kind of drama! And you're some kind of character you don't really identify with in it! So you never know what you're saying to them.

Or maybe you say you are faithful and here's how they go: They get rigid. Get struck to the core. And they say, "Who is she?"

Right? And you say — you're astounded. You say: "No. I didn't say anything about infidelity. I said fidelity. Fih. Fih." That's a bad thing about that word. You feel silly saying "Fih."

And they say, "Is she pretty?"

And you say, "No!" And then you're dead.

"Don't lie to me," she says. "Is she young?"

"She's not anything!" you say, or something. I don't

know what the fuck you say. I do know that this woman you have just been trying to share your fidelity-to-her with is now liable to say things to you that you wouldn't say to a war criminal.

Women are people who live on this gossamer plane full of blood, and then when they think you've torn it, they have these steel teeth.

There's a terrible discrepancy at work.

People say, "Men are polygamous, women monogamous." I don't think that's the difference, exactly. In fact, it scares the shit out of me. Doesn't it mean that men want to marry a whole bunch of women? I don't.

What I think is, women have it in their heads, in a kind of different way, that that is the difference and therefore they sort of think of themselves as being prepared — only they aren't — to overlook or count on certain things on the part of men that are not the things that actually happen or that men have in mind. Even though it's women that the things that do happen, happen with.

It's also women that the things that don't happen, happen with. Deep down inside, women know that. That's the trouble. But they can't comprehend it. And neither can men.

So a lot of men are faithful. A lot of men would like to be polygamous about as much as they'd like to live on five different planets at once. Which is not to deny that they may sit somewhere eating smoked almonds and thinking, "I sure would like to get laid."

I don't think women have the concept, "get laid." Men don't want them to. If women ever got it, they'd change it.

If You Can Read This,
You're Too Close

WHAT do we speak of when we speak of "literature"? Before we can begin to "answer" that question, we must ask another question: "What do we speak of when we speak of 'What'?" This is itself a peculiarly *written* question, since it cannot be asked in conversation without leading to this sort of thing:

"What?"

" 'What.' "

"*What?*"

" ' "What." ' "

"*What did you say?*"

"Are you saying, ' "*What*," did you say?' or 'What did you *say*?'?"

"No! I'm asking what *you* said."

At this point we would be forced to clarify our remarks by wiggling our fingers — now two on each hand, to signify "quote" marks, now just one on each hand, to signify so-called "single quote" marks, or, as the British call them, "inverted commas." Imagine how difficult it would be to express the statement " 'inverted commas' " (that is to say, the phrase "inverted commas" surrounded by . . .)[1] by wiggling our fingers. Especially if the conversation were literally (so to speak) Anglo-American — that is, between an Anglo, on the one hand (so to speak), and an American, on the other. The British, of course, use (') to mean (").

It was the great advance of Hercule De Mincement, in his pioneer work *Quoi qua 'Quoi,'* to show that even to say

---

1. You know what I mean.

"Wh ..." ("*Qu* ...") is to assume too much.[2] Since then we have tended to speak of " 'What,' " for argument's sake, as " '*Quoi*,' " and of the work of De Mincement and his followers as Quoism.[3]

In *Quoi qua 'Quoi'* (whose publication caused a cobblestone to be hurled at the Sorbonne, cracking a *philosophe*) appear the first of De Mincement's now classic imaginary dialogues involving Dominique You, Jean Lafitte's "right-hand man." Down in "torrid Batavia," where the "Father of Waters laves the Delta and the Gulf," Lafitte's "privateers" were "a law unto themselves," but in the "Battle of New Orleans," "rallying behind" "Andy" Jackson, they "fit the bloody British" with grand "*esprit de corps*" at a "cotton-bale barricade":

> *Behind it stood our little force —*
> *None wished it to be greater;*
> *For every man was half a horse*
> *And half an alligator.*[4]

At one time Dominique You was known to every schoolboy reader of swashbuckling tales. And yet, De Mincement points out, the doughty little cannoneer must have caused consternation in the bayous when he was asked, "Who're you?" and he answered, "I'm You."

But maybe You spoke only French. Then he may have said, "*Je suis You.*" "You are *fou*," a speaker of both languages, who assumed that You, too, was bilingual, may have replied. In print You might have cleared up the matter by

<hr>

2. De Mincement's title is drolly resistant to citation, even by a Frenchman, because even in France, "*qua*," qua Latin, should be set in roman (not to be confused with *roman*) within a title reference, since it is italicized *outside* title references. But if you don't italicize the middle word of a three-word title that is hardly conventionally titular-looking to begin with, then what — as De Mincement might put it — do you have?

3. Originally "Quoiism," but one *i* (some say the left, some the right) was, as De Mincement's colleague Achille Taupinière once put it lightly, "soon winked."

4. According to a popular song of the period.

writing (we're speaking of French print, now), "Pas '*you*,' 'You.' "[5] But You appears — in engravings of the period[6] — to have been illiterate.

De Mincement also raises the question of "*pain.*" In Anglo-American print, it is unclear whether "*pain*" (or " '*pain*' ") is being italicized for emphasis, or to show that it is French. For instance:

"My wife makes great *pain.*"

"Great *pain?*"

"Yep."

"Great *pain?* How do you mean she makes great pain?"

"Not *pain. Pain.* Homemade *pain.*"

Let's return to Dominique You. Say he is at a get-together with some strictly English speakers.

"Who're you?" one of these English speakers asks You.

"You," You replies. (He *understands* some English, just doesn't speak it.)

" 'You'? What do you mean you're me?"

"*Pas vous,*" says You, "You."

"Well pah-voo you, too," says the English speaker.

"*Non, non, non,*" says You, going for his cutlass.

The English speaker — not knowing whom he is dealing with — bristles. "See here!" he cries. "First you say you're me, then you say a lot of gibberish, then . . . I say! Who are you to take offense when I say the same thing you said to *me* back to . . . *you?*"

"*Oui! Oui!*" says You, thinking the English speaker has at last realized who he is.

"*We!?*" exclaims the English speaker, unable to imagine what this small, nasty Frog can think the two of them have in common.

There lies the crux of Quoist theory. Beyond that, there is

5. Or, more precisely: «Pas «*you*», «You».
6. One of the problems rigorous Quoism runs into, incidentally, is the impossibility, to date, of italicizing a period.

scant agreement even as to how "Quoist" is pronounced. Some feel it rhymes with "hoist." Another pronunciation may be inferred from a recent sardonic reference to De Mincement as "Jesus Quoist."[7]

"What do we speak of when we speak of 'literature'?" indeed.

And what if we should work our way all the way through "What"? We would still have "do" and "we" and "speak" and "of" and "when" and a *second*, distinct, "we" and "speak" and "of" to clear up before we got to " 'literature.' " Furthermore, in a startling paper entitled " 'Q . . .'/Cue/Queue,"[8] a brash young Johns Hopkins Englistician named John Hopkin may well have gone beyond De Mincement himself.

Experts consider it unlikely that literature, "itself," will ever catch up. Indeed a consensus is growing, among the toughest-minded of a new generation of Quoists, that literature — not to mention, as De Mincement has put it, " ' " 'literature,' " ' " (*quote[singlequote(quote-unquote)unsinglequote]unquote*)"[9] — is an illusion.

BLUE YODEL 26

MRS. AND MR. O.

MRS. O.: *I'll tell you one thing they don't tell 'em enough. They don't tell 'em, "You sure look pretty tonight, Sugar Babe," enough. Would that be hard?*

---

7. In Caesura Tax's redeconstructive prose sequence, *Tales Untold II.*
8. Delivered by mistake but to great applause before the International Polymer-Polypeptide Congress last year in Kew.
9. My translation, his italics.

MR. O.: *Aw, Sugar Babe . . .*

MRS. O.: *Don't "Sugar Babe" me.*

MR. O.: *Aww . . .*

MRS. O.: *Don't "Aww . . ." me.*

MR. O.: *Now you know sure as I do say it, you'd say, "I do not. I look like I . . ."*

MRS. O.: *I look like I what?*

MR. O.: *No! I'm saying, you'd . . . , if I . . .*

MRS. O.: *Let's just drop it.*

MR. O.: *You know, matter of fact, "You sure . . . ," I mean you sure do look . . .*

MRS. O.: *Not now! Not after I had to tell you don't say it.*

MR. O.: *Awww . . .*

MRS. O.: *Noooo. Unh-unh. Not now.*

Why I Live Where I Live, If I Do

"Why do you live where you live?" is an odd damn question. Like "Why did you show up at the Wiltses' drunk?" In the first place, I don't believe I know any people named Wilts. In the second place, one doesn't do everything by design.

Since leaving Georgia, where I grew up, I have perhaps tried to avoid being characterized — from behind, so to speak — by where I live. Mill River, Massachusetts, population roughly one hundred, where I do live, is not a well-defined place. There are two of them, for one thing. The other one is in some other county. Neither of them is on most maps. And all the TV channels we get in our Mill

River are from out of state. I sit in the Berkshire Hills in the Bay State eating homegrown collards and watching some guy who is probably from Idaho, originally, read me news of Schenectady city-council action. It keeps me from feeling like part of a target group.

I came to the Mill River area not so much because I was lured by its features, which include frequent snow up to the coccyx, but because I missed my children, who moved up this way after I got divorced. One of these young people was born just inside Queens and spent most of the first month of her life in Waxahachie, Texas. The other was conceived on Polo Drive in Atlanta and born just outside Harlem. Their stepmother was once Miss Possum International and grew up playing Monopoly in French. We all root for Pittsburgh.

My idea of where I would like to live has never been clear. No place looks so good to me as New York City just before dusk or at three o'clock in the morning. Walking in the woods is good, but there is no sin there and nothing to read. I like walking in the streets and looking at signs like META-TARSAL COOKIES in a shoe-repair window. What are meta-tarsal cookies?

Then, too, I like being in a certain size of dime store in maybe Clanton, Alabama, saying "Yes, ma'am, I bleev I do" to the saleslady, just as smooth, but privately tingling with unwonted familiarity.

I *know* I don't belong in New England, in whose entirety there is no real pork barbecue. However, here I am, former assistant coach of a relaxed, crackerjack New England Little League team, the Mill River Red Sox, which not long ago won the pennant, trounced the rest of the league's all-stars, and went on to edge an upscale Lenox nine.

What I would like, ideally, is to be bicoastal and, also, a denizen of the excluded middle. Far-flung as Phil Donahue but still hanging out on the corner. Able to make state-of-the-art remarks about tent-caterpillar control yet quite likely to have seen something in *Wet*. It's too much! It can't work! In the last scene I may find resolution in the Schizo Home, barking like a dog one minute and the next minute yelling, "Clyde! Clyde! Where's muh boots and shoes? Where's muh boots and shoes, Clyde? I think the dogs got 'em," like Gene Hackman, shot and raving in *Bonnie and Clyde*.

Or maybe I will just sort of float along.

Mill River's population has been in decline since the eighteenth century. I guess the per capita income has risen some since then but not dramatically. There haven't been any mills in Mill River to speak of since the railroad bypassed us shortly after the invention of the railroad, but there is a river, the Konkapot, which makes a sound — *konkapotkonkapotkonkapot*, only more liquid — that we can hear from our house at night. Nothing else public in town is running after six.

Our place is not precisely bucolic (a three-minute walk to town hall) or urban (next to town hall lives a cow) or suburban (a local man sold his entire lawn for topsoil a few years ago). In just over two hours by car I can be in Gotham, but on the other hand our dogs fight porcupines.

We have plenty of dogs: two. Because we live next to an expanse of woods, our dogs come home looking like porcupines and smelling like skunks. We might as well let the porcupines and the skunks themselves come on inside. One morning recently we opened the door to let the dogs in, and here came one of them barreling home from way back up the dirt road, running and beaming, running and beaming *wham* she was ambushed and knocked flying by Colonel, the neighboring husky, but scrabble roll scramble she was back up running and beaming, beaming and running, closer and closer, running beaming indoors *plangk plonk plang* she was up on top of the piano. She never did that before. And that was our more nearly ordinary dog. We are always trying to figure out what our other dog looks like. I say she looks like President Benjamin Harrison in the face and, overall, like something drawn by Hugh Lofting, author and illustrator of the Dr. Dolittle books. My wife says she looks like the Flying Nun. That's one thing to do in Mill River, sit around discussing what your dog looks like.

We also have two cats and a horse. I was once on a Peoria, Illinois, radio station, live, by telephone, standing in our kitchen. Someone I had never seen before (I had every reason to assume that Ed Murray, our neighbor, was still the complete local police force) burst in wearing a badge and said, *"Your horse is out!"*

"I'm on the radio!" I said. He didn't believe me.

"My horse is out!" I told Peoria. It seemed irrelevant. This was a sports talk show.

"He won't go far!" I assured the officer. (If he had been Ed Murray, he would have known better — our horse went down to the library once.) Satisfied, he rushed away. I still don't know why he wasn't Ed Murray. Maybe he was a Peoria policeman. But in that case how could he tell it was our horse?

"Getting back to Oakland-Houston Sunday," said the Peoria host. Who, today, *is* ever all in one place?

Let's see. No mills, a river. Excellent shopping. My main daily outing is to the Mill River Store, where I confer with Gary and Peter Broggi, storekeepers, and Addie Schwarz, who runs the post office (except on Saturdays, when it's former storekeeper Lee Barnes's wife Julie), which is housed in the store. Lee used to put customers on: when the weather was zero degrees, he would complain that the mosquitoes were giving him fits. Addie will not only give you your mail, she will also let you know that your horse has been down to the library. She had a dog once that was bit by a snake and all his organs exploded inside. For a long time, Addie thought the dog was just getting fat.

We live on the outskirts of Mill River, but it's a short-skirted town. I walk to the store in three and a half minutes.

Get the *Times*, the *Daily News*, the *Globe*. And the mail. And liquor. And manila envelopes. And produce. And lock washers. And great meat. Jim, an excellent butcher, taught Gary.

Except for having your car fixed or inspected by Jack or Eldred Stanton, that's about all there is to do right in town (I mentioned going to the library). But on our property I can always cut firewood or screw around with the compost. We have more than an acre of trees, quite a few of which are dead. Chop one of those dried-out boys down with an ax, drag it up to the house past the bemused horse, saw it up with a Swedish handsaw, split the logs with a good old American splitting maul. A person likes to *whang!* Right? Not too many opportunites to *whang*, more than enough to *be whanged*, in the city.

The satisfactions of compost are more rarefied. Compost, to me, is a lot like writing. Sometimes our heap doesn't seem to want to break down. "I like compost," I will yell at it. "But not very mulch!" Or, "Dust thou art, to dust returneth, was not spoken of my soil!" Our compost *never* — at least while I'm watching it — steams. You hear about piles that emit visible rays of heat, but that is a pleasure I've been denied. Still and all, I take pride in our down-to-earth clump of decadence. There are various ways — apparatus, structure — you can rig up your compost so it works faster. I don't get into any of that. My whole interest is *mix*.

Flat beer, bones, ashes from the wood stove, tobacco spit, coffee grounds, shredded *Timeses* and *Newses* and *Globes*, stale birthday cake, grass clippings, bad fruit, burned popcorn, struck matches, butts of cigars from Art Rooney, our horse's manure, spoiled hay, etiolated broccoli, black zucchini, lobster shells, fish eyes, the pet sand crabs that froze, mice the cats couldn't finish, olive pits, finger blood, hair from each of our combs and brushes, dish-rinse water, peels, hulls, parings, stems, twigs, leaves, bark, sawdust, eggshells, fingernail clippings, pencil sharpenings, moldy applesauce, weeds, sand, month-old bread, live worms (many of them descended from five dozen I got at Hugh Carter's worm farm in Plains), corncobs, apple cores, dust, pine straw, wine dregs, tea bags, string, crusts, crumbs, sardine oil, melon rinds, artichoke chokes, shrimp legs. A *great heterogeneity of tissues,* coming together to create a richness, like unsavory influences forming a style.

I am open to the accusation that I see compost as an end in itself. But we do grow some real red damn tomatoes such as you can't get in the stores. And potatoes, beans, lettuce, collards, onions, squash, cauliflower, eggplant, carrots, peppers. *Dirt* in your own backyard, producing things you eat. Makes you wonder.

Don't have to be on no committees in Mill River. Don't have to do no socializing without enthusiasm. Do have all these hills, vales, falls, deer, grosbeaks, and woodchucks. Low property taxes. Never have to wait for a tennis court. Right-off-the-stalk sweet corn. Kind of people around who, if you or your car turns into ice, which you or it is likely to do during at least six of the year's months, will help you get thawed. And we don't worry about burglary — we real, local residents don't. It's true, some of these city people have had their weekend places broken into. I didn't do it.

BLUE YODEL 27

JOSEPH

Now Rose says I'm too androgynous. She says she can't continue to grow unless she has somebody to bounce off of. So she made me go to this Male Empowerment Workshop. Is what they call it. Men getting together to recapture their natural male energy that they've been suppressing because it pissed women off. Now, suppressing it pisses women off.

One of the men who showed up was Jimmy Carter. But we all agreed that whatever he said was off the record, and he left early because he had to make some chairs. I'll tell you one thing, he was hip to what we'd been through. Of course you never know with politicians; he might just be after the men's vote. He was wearing this Teddy Roosevelt moustache. I don't see how a moustache can be off the record.

The first few hours, we complained. This man David said: "You do things in certain ways with women for a while, and not for very long necessarily, and it gives you a character with them. And they expect you to be that character whether they like it or not. Especially if they don't like it. It's a real question in my mind, whether women actually want you to change or they want to have somebody just about like you that they can keep telling he's got to change."

This man Bob got up and said this:

Women have gotten real tough. This woman I live with, Merrilee, is always making decisions now. "Let's move to Greece," she says. "Well," I say, "If we did that, it would involve . . ."

"If we did that," she yells. "I'm so tired of hearing if we did that. I want to do it."

So I admit, "I guess I'm too aware of all the ramifications."

"You're too something," she says. "You might as well be too thumb-up-your-ass as too aware of the ramifications, it'd be the same effect and easier on you."

"Thumb up your . . ." Where did Merrilee hear that kind of expression? That's one I never heard. Women didn't used to talk like that. Did they?

Then our group activator, who has studied with shamans, said we'd been complaining long enough. Now he said we had to dramatize our empowerment.

So he handed out these bear masks, and we did the bear

dance. And lion masks and the lion dance. And hawk masks. This one man Peter, who'd devoted his life to the peace movement until he was pushed aside as an antinuclear organizer by a woman who'd had computer and aikido training, did the hawk dance and cried.

Then we went beyond the masks and started talking about what we really wanted to do. "Go home," said Peter. But the activator talked him out of it. "Okay then," Peter said. "Get drunk."

So our group activator brought out this stuff he said was mead. It had stuff floating in it. "This is mead, huh?" said David. He poured a bottle of vodka in it. This was some of our conversation:

"One man's mead . . ."

"Another man's Pusan. You ever in Korea? Shit, in Korea, man, you got to stay so drunk —"

"Is it sideways there?"

"Korea, man, you got to stay so drunk, you can't tell."

"This what shamans drink?"

" 'Shame, shame on you. Shame, shame on you.' Spade Cooley."

"Be talkin bout no spade coolies."

"Huh? Talkin about Spade Cooley the bandleader. Western swing. Murdered his wife. Had this delusion she was screwing Roy Rogers."

"My wife had the delusion she married him. So, I tried to get the role down: A cowboy who's pure. Modest. Comes home. But takes care of business. Okay. I faked it. Then she got a sense. She got a sense, 'You're holding part of yourself back.' Next thing I know —"

"You're too quick on the Trigger! Whooooo!"

"Very funny. Very hilarila . . . rous."

"Hey! Don't feel like the Lone Ranger! Whooooo!"

"Be talkin bout no Lone Ranger, either."

"The Lone Ranger? What uffuck'd the Lone Ranger do?"

"Man ... You know what kemosabi means in Swahili?"

" 'Cowboy Who Hold Part of Self Back'?"

"Know what my wife cooks now? Erevy ... Every night. Bung means. I ming bean ... I mean bung ming ..."

"Knew a woman Bung Ming in Korea. That's when I'd get so drunk ... Get the frozen stick. You ever get the frozen stick? No feelin in it? But it won't go down? Tell old Bung Ming: 'Enjoy it, Bung Ming. Let me know when you're through. And I'll go out and drive some tent pegs with it.' "

"Hey! Be tawmbout drivin no tent ..."

"No, I'm just sayin — frozen stick. You didn'ever have the frozen stick? When you been dringin? Seems like, id be a real asset; but ... it's ... like, it's not yours. Frozen stick. Funny thing."

"A man's nature ain't funny."

"Bung means. Bing ... mungs."

Our activator said we weren't getting anywhere. We had to be focusing on what we wanted to do. So this man Eric said he always wanted to be bald. Because he heard baldness went with strong hormones. We all jumped up and did the hormone dance. Until two men, Ellis and Thorne, threw up. And we looked over and Eric was shaving his head!

"Hey, that's radical," this man Guy said. "Eric did it! Eric got bald!" And we all except Ellis and Thorne toasted Eric. And sang the — I don't know, just spontaneously we all started — we sang "The Marine Hymn."

"I'll tell you what I want to do," Guy yelled. "I want to liberate some people from some Communist Cubans!" And we were doing the liberation dance. And somebody yelled, "I want to pistol-whip some Cubans!"

And somebody else yelled, "I want to bayonet some Cubans right in their squinty yellow Commonomism-spreading teeth!"

And somebody else yelled, "What the fuck are you doing?"

And we looked over and there was Peter with his shirt off. Gluing Eric's hair onto himself. In a pattern.

"What the fuck is that?" somebody said.

"Cruciform chest hair," Peter said.

And people started saying, "Aw, shit."

And Peter said, "You know, I just . . . I just said 'cruci-form' because . . . Just, it goes across here and then a vertical line and it, well, you know, it sets off your pecs and I always wanted . . ."

Our activator, even, said, "I don't believe I'd've told that."

"I want some pussy," said Thorne, and he started crying. "And somebody to make me some soft scrambled eggs."

Ellis threw up again.

Then we all went home.

"So? How'd it go?" Rose asked me.

I said, "Oh, you know."